brilliant
Microsoft®
PowerPoint 2003
POCKET BOOK

Joe Habraken

PEARSON
Prentice
Hall

Harlow, England • London • New York • Boston • San Francisco • Toronto
Sydney • Tokyo • Singapore • Hong Kong • Seoul • Taipei • New Delhi
Cape Town • Madrid • Mexico City • Amsterdam • Munich • Paris • Milan

Pearson Education Limited
Edinburgh Gate
Harlow
Essex CM20 2JE
England

and Associated Companies throughout the world

Visit us on the World Wide Web at:
www.pearsoned.co.uk

Original edition appeared in, Microsoft® Office 2003 All-in-One, 1st edition, 0789729369 by
Joe Habraken, published by Que Publishing, Copyright © Que Publishing.

This UK edition published by PEARSON EDUCATION LTD, Copyright © 2006

ISBN-13: 978-0-13-243563-5
ISBN-10: 0-13-243563-2

British Library Cataloguing-in-Publication Data
A catalogue record for this book is available from the British Library

10 9 8 7 6 5 4 3 2 1
10 09 08 07 06

Typeset in 9.5pt Helvetica by 30
Printed and bound in Great Britain by Ashford Colour Press Ltd, Gosport, Hampshire

The Publisher's policy is to use paper manufactured from sustainable forests.

Brilliant Pocket Books

What you need to know – when you need it!

When you're working on your PC and come up against a problem that you're unsure how to solve, or want to accomplish something in an application that you aren't sure how to do, where do you look? If you are fed up with wading through pages of background information in unwieldy manuals and training guides trying to find the piece of information or advice that you need RIGHT NOW, and if you find that helplines really aren't that helpful, then Brilliant Pocket Books are the answer!

Brilliant Pocket Books have been developed to allow you to find the info that you need easily and without fuss and to guide you through each task using a highly visual step-by-step approach – providing exactly what you need to know, when you need it!

Brilliant Pocket Books are concise, easy-to-access guides to all of the most common important and useful tasks in all of the applications in the Office 2003 suite. Short, concise lessons make it really easy to learn any particular feature, or master any task or problem that you will come across in day-to-day use of the applications.

When you are faced with any task on your PC, whether major or minor, that you are unsure about, your Brilliant Pocket Book will provide you with the answer – almost before you know what the question is!

Contents

Introduction

Welcome to the *Brilliant Microsoft® PowerPoint Pocket Book* – a handy visual quick reference that will give you a basic grounding in the common features and tasks that you will need to master to use Microsoft® PowerPoint 2003 in any day-to-day situation. Keep it on your desk, in your briefcase or bag – or even in your pocket! – and you will always have the answer to hand for any problem or task that you come across.

Find out what you need to know – when you need it!

You don't have to read this book in any particular order. It is designed so that you can jump in, get the information you need and jump out – just look up the task in the contents list, turn to the right page, read the introduction, follow the step-by-step instructions – and you're done!

How this book works

Each section in this book includes foolproof step-by-step instructions for performing specific tasks, using screenshots to illustrate each step. Additional information is included to help increase your understanding and develop your skills – these are identified by the following icons:

 Jargon buster – New or unfamiliar terms are defined and explained in plain English to help you as you work through a section.

 Timesaver tip – These tips give you ideas that cut corners and confusion. They also give you additional information related to the topic that you are currently learning. Use them to expand your knowledge of a particular feature or concept.

 Important – This identifies areas where new users often run into trouble, and offers practical hints and solutions to these problems.

Brilliant Pocket Books are a handy, accessible resource that you will find yourself turning to time and time again when you are faced with a problem or an unfamiliar task and need an answer at your fingertips – or in your pocket!

1 Working in PowerPoint

In this lesson, you learn how to start and exit PowerPoint. You also learn about the PowerPoint presentation window.

→ Starting PowerPoint

PowerPoint is a powerful application that enables you to create presentations that can be viewed on a computer. Using PowerPoint, you can print handouts or create film slides for a presentation. PowerPoint also enables you to add animation and sound to your presentations, which makes it the perfect tool for business presentations or classroom lectures.

To start PowerPoint, follow these steps:

1. Click the **Start** button.
2. Move your mouse pointer to **Programs** (**All Programs** on Windows XP). A menu of programs appears. Point at the **Microsoft Office** icon.
3. Move your mouse pointer to the **Microsoft Office PowerPoint** icon and click it. The PowerPoint application window opens, as shown in Figure 1.1.

The first thing you see when you open PowerPoint is that the application window is divided into different areas. The default view for PowerPoint is the Normal view (you learn about the different PowerPoint views in Lesson 3, "Working with Slides in Different Views"). On the left of the screen is a pane that can be used to switch between an Outline and Slides view of the current presentation. In the center of the PowerPoint application window is the Slide pane; this is where you work individually on each slide in the presentation.

Below the Slide pane is the Notes pane, which enables you to add notes to the presentation for each slide. On the far right of the application window is the New Presentation task pane. The task pane provides different commands and features depending on what you are currently doing in PowerPoint.

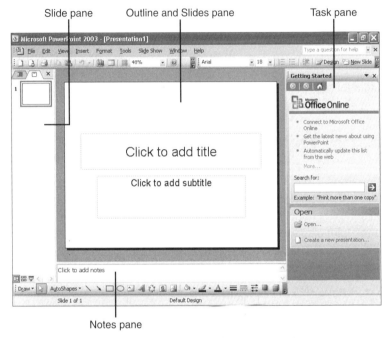

Figure 1.1 **The PowerPoint window is divided into several panes.**

→ Getting Comfortable with the PowerPoint Window

Although PowerPoint looks a little different from the other Office applications, such as Word and Excel, all the standard Office application components, such as the menu bar and various toolbars, are available to you as you design your presentations. The basic element of a presentation is a slide, to which you add text and other objects, such as images, using the Slide pane (which is discussed in the next lesson). PowerPoint provides several slide layouts; each layout provides the necessary text boxes or clip-art boxes for creating a particular type of slide.

Adding text to a slide is very straightforward. Each slide that you add to a presentation (Lesson 5, "Inserting, Deleting, and Copying Slides," discusses inserting slides into a presentation) contains placeholder text that tells you what to type into a particular text box on the slide. For example, Figure 1.2 shows a title slide. Note that the top text box on the slide says Click to Add Title.

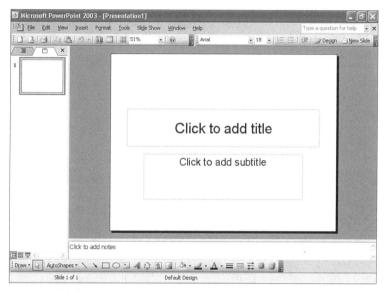

Figure 1.2 Click the placeholder text to input text into a slide.

To replace the placeholder text with your own text, just click the placeholder text. Then, you can type your entry into that text box.

Because a presentation consists of several slides, PowerPoint provides a thumbnail view of each slide in the presentation to the left of the Slides pane. Figure 1.3 shows an example of a complete presentation with a series of these thumbnail slides. This view can be used to keep track of your slides as you add them to the presentation and can even be used to rearrange slides in the presentation.

Because presentations require a certain logical arrangement of information, you can view the slides in the presentation as an outline. This enables you to make sure that you have the facts presented by each slide in the proper order for the presentation. The Outline pane also enables you to move topics within the presentation and even move information from slide to slide. Figure 1.4 shows the Outline pane for a presentation that contains several slides.

Thumbnail slide images

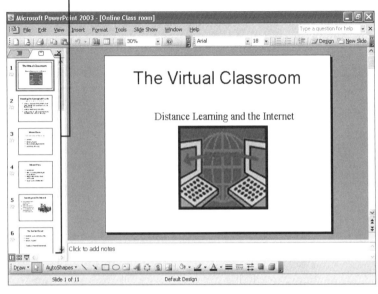

Figure 1.3 The Slides pane enables you to view thumbnails of the slides in the presentation.

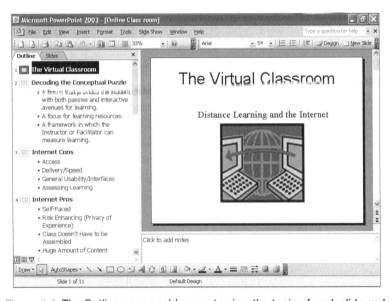

Figure 1.4 The Outline pane enables you to view the topic of each slide and each piece of text information included in a slide.

You learn about using the Slides and Outline pane in Lesson 3, "Working with Slides in Different Views."

Lesson 3 shows you how you can edit the presentation's text in either the Outline or the Slide pane. Changes in one pane are reflected in the other pane. When you want to place a nontext object on a slide (such as a graphic), you do so in the Slide pane.

→ Exiting PowerPoint

When you finish using PowerPoint, you can exit the application. This closes any open presentations (PowerPoint might prompt you to save changes to those presentations).

To exit PowerPoint, perform one of the following:

- Click the PowerPoint window's **Close (X)** button.
- Double-click the **Control Menu** icon in the left corner of the title bar, or click it once to open the Control menu and then select Close.
- Open the **File** menu and select **Exit**.
- Press **Alt+F4**.

2 Creating a New Presentation

In this lesson, you learn several ways to create a presentation. You also learn how to save, close, and open an existing presentation.

→ Starting a New Presentation

PowerPoint offers several ways to create a new presentation. Before you begin, decide which method is right for you:

- The AutoContent Wizard offers the highest degree of help. It walks you through each step of creating the new presentation. When you're finished, you have a standardized group of slides, all with a similar look and feel, for a particular situation. Each slide created includes dummy text that you can replace with your own text.

- A design template provides a professionally designed color, background, and font scheme that applies to the slides you create yourself. It does not provide sample slides.

- You can also start a new presentation based on an existing presentation. This "copies" all the slides in the existing presentation and allows you to save the new presentation under a new filename.

- You can start from scratch and create a totally blank presentation. That means that you build the presentation from the ground up and create each slide in the presentation. (Beginners might want to use the wizard or templates until they get a feel for the overall design approach used to create a cohesive slide presentation.)

Jargon buster

Design Template A design template is a preformatted presentation file (without any slides in it). When you select a template, PowerPoint applies the color scheme and general layout of the template to each slide you create for the presentation.

With the AutoContent Wizard, you select the type of presentation you want to create (such as corporate, sales, or various projects), and PowerPoint creates an outline for the presentation.

The following steps describe how you use the AutoContent Wizard:

1 Select the **File** menu and select **New**. The New Presentation task pane appears on the right of the PowerPoint window, as shown in Figure 2.1 (if the Presentation task pane was already open in the window, you can skip to step 2).

Figure 2.1 **Start the AutoContent Wizard from the task pane.**

2 Click the **From AutoContent Wizard** link on the task pane.

3 The AutoContent Wizard starts. The opening wizard screen summarizes the process you should follow to create a new presentation. Click **Next** to continue.

4 The wizard provides you with category buttons for different categories of presentations: General, Corporate, Projects, and Sales/Marketing. Select a category by selecting the appropriate button (see Figure 2.2). A list of specific presentations will appear to the right of the category buttons. To see all the AutoContent presentations available, click the **All** button.

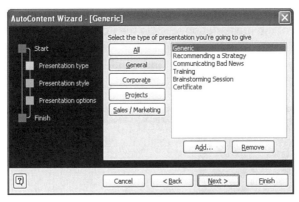

Figure 2.2 **Select a category button to view a list of presentation types.**

5 After selecting a particular category of presentations, select a presentation type in the list provided. You can choose to create a generic presentation, or presentations recommending a strategy, communicating bad news, or for a brainstorming session (among others). After selecting the type of presentation (I selected generic), click **Next** to continue.

6 On the next screen, you select how you will give the presentation. Select one of the following options:

- **Onscreen Presentation**—Choose this if you plan to use a computer and your PowerPoint file to present the show.

- **Web Presentation**—Choose this if you are planning to distribute the presentation as a self-running or user-interactive show.

- **Black-and-White Overheads**—Choose this if you plan to make black-and-white transparencies for your show.

- **Color Overheads**—Choose this if you plan to make color transparencies for your show.

- **35mm Slides**—Choose this if you plan to send your PowerPoint presentation to a service bureau to have 35mm slides made. (You probably don't have such expensive and specialized equipment in your own company.)

7 After selecting how you will give the presentation, click **Next** to continue.

8 On the next screen, type the presentation title into the text box provided (see Figure 2.3). If you want to add a footer (such as your name or other) that will appear at the bottom of each slide of the presentation, click in the Footer box and type the appropriate text. If you do not want a date and/or slide number on each slide, deselect the **Date Last Updated** and/or **Slide Number** check boxes.

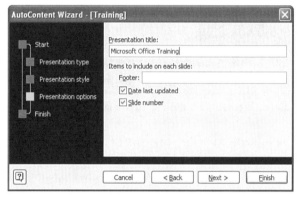

Provide a title for the presentation.

9 After supplying the presentation title and any optional information, click **Next** to continue.

10 PowerPoint takes you to the last wizard screen, where you should simply click **Finish**.

The title slide of your new presentation appears in the Slide pane. The entire presentation, including the dummy text placed on each slide, appears in the Outline pane on the left of the PowerPoint window (see Figure 2.4).

You can start working on your presentation right away by replacing the dummy text on the slides with your own text. Just select the existing text in a text box and type right over it. You learn about editing text in slide text boxes in Lesson 7, "Adding and Modifying Slide Text."

Creating a New Presentation with a Design Template

A template is the middle ground between maximum hand-holding (the AutoContent Wizard) and no help at all (Blank Presentation). Two kinds of templates are available: presentation templates and design templates.

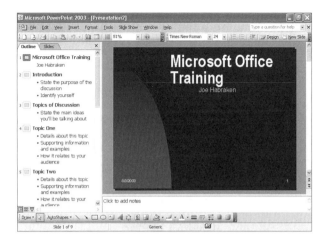

Figure 2.4 **Your new presentation appears in the PowerPoint window.**

When you use the AutoContent Wizard, you use a presentation template. It contains not only formatting, but also sample slides that contain placeholder text. The other kind of template is a design template. It contains the overall formatting for the slides of the presentation but does not actually create any slides. If you want to use a presentation template that includes placeholder text, use the AutoContent Wizard, as explained in the preceding section.

To start a new presentation using a design template, follow these steps:

1 Select the **File** menu and select **New**. The New Presentation task pane appears on the right of the PowerPoint window.

Timesaver tip

Select Your Task Pane   If the task pane is already open for another PowerPoint feature, click the drop-down arrow on its title bar and select **New Presentation** from the list that appears.

2 On the New Presentation task pane, click the **From Design Template** link. PowerPoint switches to the Slide Design side pane, which displays a list of design templates, as shown in Figure 2.5. A blank title slide for the presentation appears in the Slide pane.

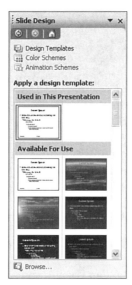

Figure 2.5 Design templates are listed in the task pane.

3 Click a template from the Available For Use section of the task pane. PowerPoint then formats the title slide in the Slide pane using the selected template.

You can select different templates to determine the best look for your presentation. When you have found the design template that you want to use, you can immediately start working on the slides for the presentation.

Timesaver tip

The Next Step? Add more slides by clicking the **New Slide** button on the toolbar. Inserting slides into a presentation is covered in Lesson 5, "Inserting, Deleting, and Copying Slides."

Creating a New Presentation from an Existing Presentation

Another alternative for creating a new presentation is to use an existing presentation. This creates a copy of the existing presentation (and all its slides) and allows you to quickly save the presentation under a new filename.

1 Select the **File** menu and select **New**. The New Presentation task pane appears on the right of the PowerPoint window.

2 Select **From Existing Presentation** in the New Presentation task pane. The New from Existing Presentation dialog box opens (see Figure 2.6).

3 Use the Look in drop-down list to locate the drive and the folder that holds the existing presentation. When you locate the existing presentation, select it and then click **Create New**.

4 A "copy" of the existing presentation will open in the PowerPoint window.

Figure 2.6 Open the existing presentation that the new presentation will be based on.

When you have the copy of the existing presentation open, you can edit it as needed. You can then save the presentation under a new filename as discussed later in this lesson.

Timesaver tip

What Is the Photo Album? An additional choice, Photo Album, appears on the New Presentation task pane. This new presentation option provides you with a quick way to create a presentation that contains pictures and other images. We discuss the Photo Album in Lesson 9, "Adding Graphics to a Slide."

Creating a Blank Presentation

Your fourth option for creating a new presentation is to create a blank presentation. This means that you have to create all the slides from scratch. A design for the slides can then be selected using the Slide Design task pane. You open this task pane by selecting **Format**, **Slide Design**. In the Slide Design task pane, be sure that the Design Templates icon is selected.

 Creating a new, blank presentation takes only a click: Click the **New** button on the Standard toolbar or click the **Blank Presentation** link on the New Presentation task pane. The new presentation appears in the PowerPoint window. A blank title slide is ready for you to edit.

→ Saving a Presentation

After you create a new presentation, it makes sense to save it. To save a presentation for the first time, follow these steps:

 1 Select **File**, **Save**, or just click the **Save** button on the Standard toolbar. The Save As dialog box appears (see Figure 2.7).

2 In the **File Name** text box, type the name you want to assign to the presentation. Your filenames can be as long as 255 characters and can include spaces.

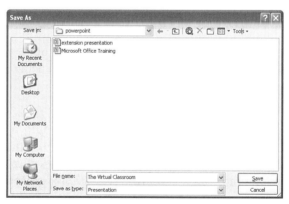

Figure 2.7 **Type a name for your presentation into the Save As dialog box.**

3 The Save In box shows in which folder the file will be saved. The default is My Documents. To select a different drive location for the file, click the **Save In** drop-down arrow and select one from the list that appears. To save to a specific folder in the drive location you've selected, double-click the folder in which you want to store the file.

4 Click **Save**.

2

Now that you have named the file and saved it to a disk, you can save any changes you make simply by pressing **Ctrl+S** or clicking the **Save** button on the Standard toolbar. Your data is saved under the filename you assigned to the presentation in the Save As dialog box.

To create a copy of a presentation under a different filename or location, select **File**, **Save As**. The Save As dialog box reappears; follow steps 2 to 4 as discussed in this section to give the file a new name or location.

→ Closing a Presentation

You can close a presentation at any time. Note that although this closes the presentation window, it does not exit PowerPoint as do the methods discussed in Lesson 1. To close a presentation, follow these steps:

1 If more than one presentation is open, click a presentation's button on the Windows taskbar to make it the active presentation, or you can select the **Window** menu and select the presentation from the list provided.

2 Select **File**, **Close**, or click the presentation's **Close** (**X**) button. (It's the lower of the two Close buttons; the upper one is for the PowerPoint window.) If you haven't saved the presentation or if you haven't saved since you last made changes, a dialog box appears, asking whether you want to save.

3 To save your changes, click **Yes**. If this is a new presentation that has never been saved, refer to the steps in the preceding section for saving a presentation. If you have saved the file previously, the presentation window closes.

→ Opening a Presentation

A presentation, like Rome, is not built in a day, so you will probably fine-tune a presentation over time. To open a saved presentation file that you want to work on, follow these steps:

1 Select **File**, **Open**, or click the **Open** button on the Standard toolbar. The Open dialog box appears (see Figure 2.8).

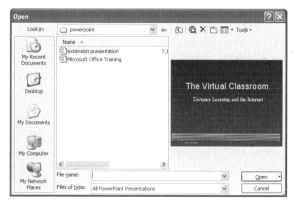

Figure 2.8 **Select the presentation you want to open.**

2 If the file isn't in the currently displayed folder, select the **Look In** drop-down arrow to choose from a list of other drives and/or folders.

3 Browse to the location containing the file and double-click it to open it in PowerPoint.

→ Finding a Presentation File

If you're having trouble locating your file, PowerPoint can help you look. Follow these steps to find a file:

1 Select **File**, **Open** (if the Open dialog box is not already open).

2 Click the **Tools** drop-down button in the Open dialog box and select **Search**. The File Search dialog box appears (see Figure 2.9).

3 In the **Search Text** box, type text that is contained in the presentation's filename. Use the Search In box to specify where you want the search to be conducted. In the Results Should Be box, specify the file types you want to be included in the search.

4 When you are ready to conduct the search, click the **Search** button.

5 Files that meet the search criteria are listed in the Results box (if you see your file in the Results box and the search is continuing, click the **Stop** button).

Figure 2.9 Use the File Search dialog box to find a presentation on your computer.

6 To open a file in the Results box, double-click the filename.

7 You are returned to the Open dialog box with the file listed in the File Name box. Click **OK** to open the file. A PowerPoint presentation then opens in the PowerPoint window.

3 Working with Slides in Different Views

In this lesson, you learn how to display a presentation in different views and how to edit slides in the Outline and Slide views.

→ Understanding PowerPoint's Different Views

PowerPoint can display your presentation in different views. Each of these views is designed for you to perform certain tasks as you create and edit a presentation. For example, Normal view has the Outline/Slides, Slide, and Notes panes; it provides an ideal environment for creating your presentation slides and for quickly viewing the organization of the slides or the information in the presentation (using the Outline or the Slides tabs). Another view, the Slide Sorter view, enables you to quickly rearrange the slides in the presentation (and is similar to the Slides view that shares the pane with the Outline tab when you are in the Normal view).

To change views, open the **View** menu and choose the desired view: **Normal**, **Slide Sorter**, **Slide Show**, or **Notes Page**.

- Normal—The default, three-pane view (which is discussed in Lesson 1, "Working in PowerPoint").

- Slide Sorter—This view shows all the slides as thumbnails so that you can easily rearrange them by dragging slides to new positions in the presentation (Figure 3.1 shows the Slide Sorter).

- Slide Show—A specialized view that enables you to preview and present your show onscreen. It enables you to test the presentation as you add slides, and it is used later when your presentation is complete.

- Notes Page—This view provides a large pane for creating notes for your speech. You can also type these notes in Normal view, but Notes Page view gives you more room and allows you to concentrate on your note text.

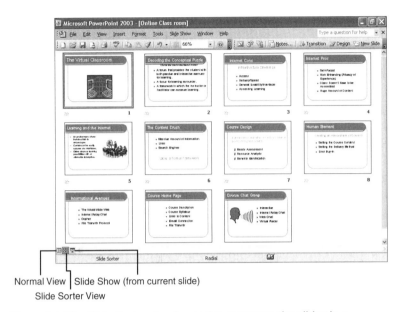

Normal View | Slide Show (from current slide)
Slide Sorter View

Figure 3.1 **The Slide Sorter view is used to rearrange the slides in a presentation.**

An even faster way to switch to certain views is to use the view buttons that are provided along the lower-left corner of the PowerPoint window. These buttons, from left to right, are Normal View, Slide Sorter View, and Slide Show (from current slide) button. A button not provided for the Notes view.

→ Moving from Slide to Slide

PowerPoint provides several ways to move from slide to slide in the presentation. The particular view you are in somewhat controls the procedure for moving to a specific slide.

In the Normal view, you can move from slide to slide using these techniques:

- Click the **Outline** tab on the far left of the window. To go to a particular slide in the outline, click the slide icon next to the slide number (see Figure 3.2). The slide opens in the Slide pane.

- Press the **Page Up** or **Page Down** keys to move to the previous or next slide, respectively.

- Click the **Previous Slide** or **Next Slide** button just below the vertical scrollbar (refer to Figure 3.2), or drag the scroll box inside the vertical scrollbar until the desired slide number is displayed.

- Click the **Slides** tab on the far left of the PowerPoint window. This enables you to move from slide to slide in the Normal view by selecting a particular slide's thumbnail. When you click the thumbnail, the slide appears in the Slide pane.

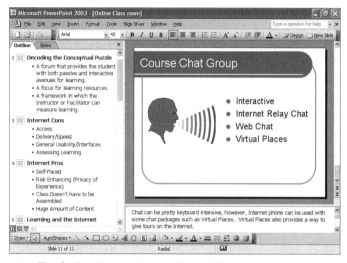

Figure 3.2 The Outline view can be used to quickly move to a particular slide.

You can also move from slide to slide in other views, such as the Slide Sorter view or the Slide Show view. In the Slide Sorter view (refer to Figure 3.1), just click a slide's thumbnail to move to that slide. You then can use any of the tools that PowerPoint provides to format the selected slide (or delete it). If you want to actually open a slide when you are working in the Slide Sorter view, so that you can edit the text it contains, double-click the slide. You are returned to the Normal view.

When you are actually showing a presentation in the Slide Show view, you can use the **Page Up** or **Page Down** keys to move from slide to slide (unless you have set up timers to change slides). You can also click a slide with the mouse to move to the next slide. You learn more about the Slide Show view in Lesson 12, "Presenting an Onscreen Slideshow."

→ Introduction to Inserting Slide Text

If you created a presentation in Lesson 2 using the AutoContent Wizard, you already have a presentation that contains several slides, but they won't contain the text you want to use. Slides created by the wizard contain placeholder text that you must replace. If you created a blank presentation or based a new presentation on a design template, you have only a title slide in that presentation, which, of course, needs to be personalized for your particular presentation. This means that additional slides will need to be added to the presentation. Lesson 5, "Inserting, Deleting, and Copying Slides," covers the creation of new slides for a presentation.

The sections that follow in this lesson look at the basics of inserting text into the text boxes provided on slides. You will look at adding new text boxes and formatting text in text boxes in Lesson 7, "Adding and Modifying Slide Text." Upcoming lessons also discuss how to add pictures and other objects to your PowerPoint slides.

Jargon buster

Object An object is any item on a slide, including text, graphics, and charts.

→ Editing Text in the Slide Pane

The text on your slides resides within boxes (all objects appear on a slide in their own boxes for easy manipulation). As shown in Figure 3.3, to edit text on a slide, click the text box to select it and then click where you want the insertion point moved, or select the text you want to replace.

When you work with the Slide pane, you might want to close the Outline/Slides pane. Just click the pane's **Close** button (X) to provide the Slide pane with the entire PowerPoint window (refer to Figure 3.3). In Lesson 7, "Adding and Modifying Slide Text," you'll learn more about adding text to a slide, including creating your own text boxes on a slide.

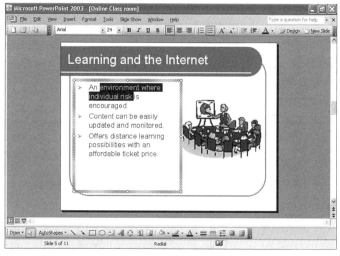

Figure 3.3 You can edit your text directly on the slide in the Slide pane.

Timesaver tip

Opening the Outline Pane If you close the Outline pane to concentrate on the Slide pane, click **View**, **Normal (Restore Panes)** to restore it to the application window.

Editing Text in the Outline Pane

The Outline pane provides another way to edit text in a slide. To switch to the Outline view on the Outline/Slides pane, click the **Outline** tab. You simply click to move the insertion point where you want it (or select the range of text you want to replace) in the outline, and then type your text (see Figure 3.4). If you've placed the insertion point in the slide text (without selecting a range), press the **Delete** key to delete characters to the right of the insertion point or press the **Backspace** key to delete characters to the left. If you've selected a range of text, either of these keys deletes the text. If you want to move the highlighted text, simply drag it to where you want it moved.

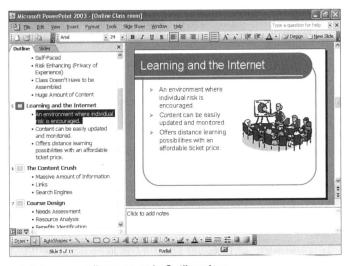

Figure 3.4 **You can edit your text in Outline view.**

Moving Text in the Outline Pane

As you work in the Normal view, you can also view your presentation slides as an outline using the Outline pane. This provides you with a quick way to move text items around on a slide or move them from slide to slide. Just select the text and drag it to a new position.

As already mentioned, you can also drag text from one slide to another. All you have to do is select a line of text in the Outline pane and drag it to another slide. You can also move a slide in the Outline pane. Drag the slide's icon in the Outline pane to a new position (under the heading for another slide).

If you aren't that confident with your dragging skills, PowerPoint provides you with help in the form of the Outlining toolbar. It provides buttons that make it easy to move text up or down on a slide (with respect to other text on the slide) or to move a slide up or down in the presentation.

3

To turn on the Outlining toolbar, right-click one of the PowerPoint toolbars and select **Outlining**. Figure 3.5 shows the Outlining toolbar on the left side of the Outline pane (the Outline pane has also been expanded to take up more of the PowerPoint window).

- To move a paragraph or text line up in a slide, select it and click the **Move Up** button.

- To move a paragraph or text down in a slide, select it and click the **Move Down** button.

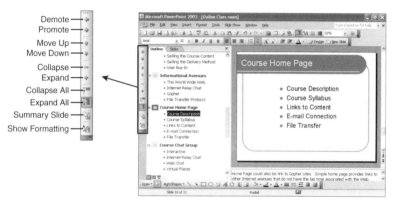

Figure 3.5 You can use the Outlining toolbar to move text and slides in the presentation.

You can also use the **Move Up** and **Move Down** buttons to move entire slides up or down in the presentation. Click the slide's icon and then use the appropriate button (it might take several clicks to move a slide up or down with respect to another slide).

If you want to see how the text is actually formatted on the slides that you are viewing in the Outline pane, click the **Show Formatting** button on the Outlining toolbar. Viewing the text as it is formatted can help you determine where the text should appear on a slide as you move the text (or whether you will have to reformat the text later).

Rearranging Text in the Outline Pane

As you can see from Figure 3.5, your presentation is organized in a multilevel outline format. The slides are at the top level of the outline, and each slide's contents are subordinate under that slide. Some slides have multiple levels of subordination (for example, a bulleted list within a bulleted list).

You can easily change an object's level in Outline view with the Tab key or the Outlining toolbar:

- To demote a paragraph in the outline, click the text, and then press the **Tab** key or click the **Demote** button on the Outlining toolbar.

- To promote a paragraph in the outline, click the text, and then press **Shift+Tab** or click the **Promote** button on the Outlining toolbar.

In most cases, subordinate items on a slide appear as items in a bulleted list. In Lesson 8, "Creating Columns and Lists," you learn how to change the appearance of the bullet and the size and formatting of text for each entry, as well as how much the text is indented for each level.

Timesaver tip

Create Summary Slides in the Outline Pane   If you would like to create a summary slide for your presentation that contains the headings from several slides, select those slides in the Outline pane (click the first slide, and then hold down the **Shift** key and click the last slide you want to select). Then, click the **Summary Slide** button on the Outlining toolbar. A new slide appears at the beginning of the selected slides containing the headings from the selected slides. You then can position the Summary slide anywhere in the presentation as you would any other slide.

4 Changing a Presentation's Look

In this lesson, you learn various ways to give your presentation a professional and consistent look.

→ Giving Your Slides a Professional Look

PowerPoint comes with dozens of professionally created designs and color schemes that you can apply to your presentations. These designs include background patterns, color choices, font choices, and more. When you apply a design template to your presentation, it applies its formatting to a special slide called the Slide Master.

The Slide Master is not really a slide, but it looks like one. It is a master design grid that you make changes to; these changes affect every slide in the presentation. When you apply a template, you are actually applying the template to the Slide Master, which in turn applies it to each slide in the presentation.

Jargon buster

Master Slide A slide that contains the master layout and color scheme for the slides in a presentation.

You don't have to work with the Slide Master itself when you apply template or color scheme changes to your presentations. Just be aware that you can open the Slide Master (select **View**, point at **Master**, and then select **Slide Master**) and change the style and fonts used by the text boxes in a presentation (see Figure 4.1). You can also select a custom background color for the slides in the presentation. Any changes that you make to the Slide Master affect all the slides in the presentation.

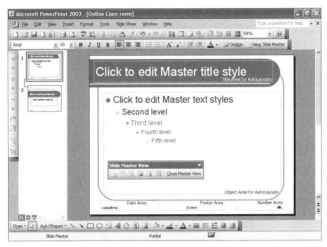

Figure 4.1 The Slide Master holds the default design and color options for the entire presentation.

You will probably find that PowerPoint provides enough template and color scheme options that you won't need to format the Slide Master itself very often. Edit its properties only if you have a very strict formatting need for the presentation that isn't covered in the templates and color schemes provided. For example, one good reason to edit the Slide Master would be a situation in which you want a graphic to appear on every slide (such as a company logo); you can place the image on the Slide Master instead of pasting it onto each slide individually.

Timesaver tip

Close the Slide Master   If you open the Slide Master, you can close it by clicking **Close Master View** on the Master View toolbar.

→ Applying a Different Design Template

You can apply a different template to your presentation at any time, no matter how you originally created the presentation. To change the design template, follow these steps:

1 Select **Format**, **Slide Design** to open the Slide Design task pane. Then, if necessary, click the **Design Templates** icon at the top of the task pane. This provides a listing of PowerPoint's many design templates (see Figure 4.2).

2 Click the template that you want to use in the list. The template is immediately applied to the slide in the Slide pane.

3 When you have decided on a particular template (you can click on any number of templates to see how they affect your slides), save the presentation (click the **Save** button on the toolbar).

Figure 4.2 Choose a different template from the Design Templates task pane.

> ## Important
>
> **The Design Template Changes Custom Formatting** If you spent time bolding text items on a slide or changing font colors, these changes are affected (lost) when you select a new design template. For example, if you have customized bold items in black in your original design template and switch to another template that uses white text, you lose your customizations. You should choose your design template early in the process of creating your presentation. Then, you can do any customized formatting at the end of the process so that it is not affected by a design template change.

When you work with design templates, you can apply them to all the slides in the presentation (as discussed in the steps provided in this section), or you can apply the template to selected slides in the presentation. Follow these steps to apply a template to a selected group of slides in a presentation:

1 Switch to the Slide Sorter view (select **View**, **Slide Sorter**).

2 Open the Slide Design task pane as outlined in the previous steps.

3 Now you must select the slide (or slides) to which you want to apply the template. Click the first slide you want to select, and then hold down the **Ctrl** key as you click other slides you want to select. To select a series of slides, click the first one and then Shift+click on the last slide to select them all.

4 Point at the design template you want to use in the Slide Design task pane; a drop-down arrow appears.

5 Click the template's drop-down arrow and select **Apply to Selected Slides** (see Figure 4.3).

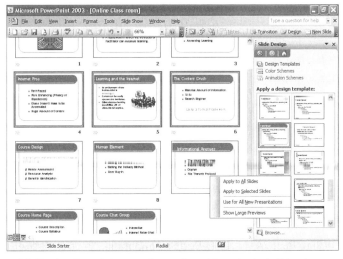

Figure 4.3 Design templates can be assigned to selected slides in a presentation.

The template's design is then applied to the selected slides.

Timesaver tip

View a Larger Design Sample To expand the view of the design templates, click the drop-down arrow on the template and select **Show Large Previews**.

→ Using Color Schemes

Design templates enable you to change the overall design and color scheme applied to the slides in the presentation (or selected slides in the presentation, as discussed in the previous section). If you like the overall design of the slides in the presentation but would like to explore some other color options, you can select a different color scheme for the particular template that you are using.

The number of color schemes available for a particular design template depends on the template itself. Some templates provide only three or four color schemes, whereas other templates provide more. As with design templates, you can assign a new color scheme to all the slides in the presentation or to selected slides.

To change the color scheme for the presentation or selected slides, follow these steps:

1. In the Normal or Slide Sorter view (use the Slide Sorter view if you want to change the color scheme for selected slides), open the task pane by selecting **View**, **Task Pane** (if the task pane is already open, skip to the next step).

2. Select the task pane's drop-down arrow and then select **Slide Design-Color Schemes**. This switches to the Color Schemes section of the Slide Design task pane. The color schemes available for the design template that you are using appear in the Apply a Color Scheme section (see Figure 4.4).

3. (Optional) If you are in the Slide Sorter view and want to assign a new color scheme only to selected slides, select those slides (click the first slide and then hold down **Ctrl** and click additional slides).

4. To assign the new color scheme to all the slides in the presentation, click a scheme in the Slide Design task pane. If you are assigning the color scheme only to selected slides, point at the color scheme and click its drop-down arrow. Select **Apply to Selected Slides**.

The new color scheme is applied to the slides in the presentation (or selected slides in the presentation). If you decide you don't like the color scheme, select another scheme from the task pane.

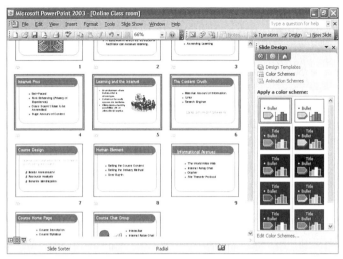

Figure 4.4 You can choose from a list of color schemes for the presentation or selected slides.

→ Changing the Background Fill

You can also fine-tune the color scheme that you add to a slide or slides by changing the background fill. This works best in cases where the design template and color scheme that you selected don't provide a background color for the slide or slides. You must be careful, however, because you don't want to pick a background color that obscures the text and graphics that you place on the slide or slides.

To change the background fill on a slide or slides, follow these steps:

1 Switch to the Slide Sorter view (select **View**, **Slide Sorter**).

2 (Optional) If you are going to change the background fill for selected slides, select those slides in the Slide Sorter window.

3 Select the **Format** menu and then select **Background**. The Background dialog box appears (see Figure 4.5).

4 Click the drop-down arrow at the bottom of the dialog box and choose a fill color from the color palette that appears.

5 To assign the fill color to all the slides in the presentation, click **Apply to All**. To assign the fill color to selected slides (if you selected slides in step 2), click **Apply**.

Figure 4.5 Use the Background dialog box to add a fill color to a slide or slides.

5 | Inserting, Deleting, and Copying Slides

In this lesson, you learn how to insert new slides, delete slides, and copy slides in a presentation.

→ Inserting Slides into a Presentation

You can insert slides into your presentation. You can insert blank slides or you can insert slides from other presentations.

Let's look at inserting blank slides. Then we can look at inserting existing slides from another presentation.

Inserting a New, Blank Slide

You can insert a slide into a presentation at any time and at any position in the presentation. To insert a new slide, follow these steps:

1 On the Outline or Slides pane, select the slide that appears just before the place where you want to insert the new slide (you can also insert a new slide in the Slide Sorter view, if you want).

2 Choose the **Insert** menu and then **New Slide**, or click the **New Slide** button on the PowerPoint toolbar. A new blank slide appears in the PowerPoint window, along with the Slide Layout task pane (see Figure 5.1).

3 In the Slide Layout task pane, select the slide layout that you want to use for the new slide. Several text slide layouts and layouts for slides that contain graphics are provided.

4 Follow the directions indicated on the slide in the Slide pane to add text or other objects. For text boxes, you click an area to select it and then type in your text. For other object placeholders, you double-click the placeholder.

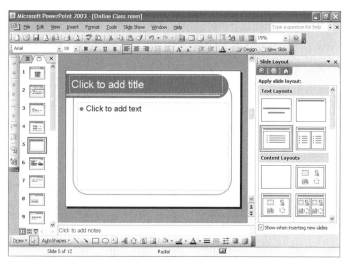

Figure 5.1 **Your new slide appears in the PowerPoint window.**

Timesaver tip

Cloning a Slide   To create an exact replica of an existing slide (in any view), select the slide you want to duplicate. Click **Insert** and then select **Duplicate Slide**. The new slide is inserted after the original slide. You can then choose a different layout for the slide if you want.

Inserting Slides from Another Presentation

If you want to insert some or all of the slides from another presentation into the current presentation, perform these steps:

1 Open the presentation into which you want to insert the slides.

2 Select the slide located before the position where you want to insert the slides.

3 Select the **Insert** menu and select **Slides from Files**. The Slide Finder dialog box appears (see Figure 5.2).

4 Click the **Browse** button to display the Browse dialog box. In the Browse dialog box, locate the presentation that contains the slides that you want to insert into the current presentation (use the **Look In** drop-down arrow to switch drives, if necessary).

5 When you locate the presentation, double-click it.

Figure 5.2 Use the Slide Finder dialog box to insert slides from another presentation.

6 The slides in the presentation appear in the Slide Finder's Select Slides box. To select the slides that you want to insert into the current presentation, click the first slide and then hold down **Ctrl** and click any subsequent slides.

7 When you have selected all the slides you want to insert, click **Insert** (if you want to insert all the slides, click **Insert All**).

8 PowerPoint inserts the slides into the presentation at the point you originally selected. Click **OK** to close the Slide Finder dialog box.

→ Creating Slides from a Document Outline

If you have created a document in Word that includes outline-style headings and numbered or bulleted lists, PowerPoint can pull the headings and the text from the document and create slides. To create slides from a document outline, follow these steps:

1 Choose the **Insert** menu, and then choose **Slides from Outline**. The Insert Outline dialog box appears (it is similar to the Open dialog box used to open a presentation or other file).

2 Use the **Insert Outline** dialog box to locate the document file you want to use.

3 Double-click the name of the document file.

PowerPoint then uses all the first-level headings to create slides for your presentation. Any text in the document below a first-level outline heading is added to the slide in an additional text box.

→ Deleting Slides

You can delete a slide from any view. To delete a slide, perform the following steps:

1. Select the slide you want to delete. You can delete multiple slides by selecting more than one slide (on the Outline or Slides pane or in the Slide Sorter view).

2. Choose the **Edit** menu, and then choose **Delete Slide**. The slide is removed from the presentation.

Timesaver tip

Use the Delete Key You can quickly delete slides by selecting the slide or slides and then pressing the **Delete** key on the keyboard.

Important

Oops! If you deleted a slide by mistake, you can get it back. Select **Edit, Undo**, or press **Ctrl+Z**. This works only if you do it immediately. You cannot undo the change if you exit PowerPoint and restart the application.

→ Cutting, Copying, and Pasting Slides

In Lesson 6, "Rearranging Slides in a Presentation," you learn how to rearrange slides using the Slide Sorter and the Outline/Slides pane. Although dragging slides to new positions in the Slide Sorter is probably the easiest way to move slides, you can use the **Cut**, **Copy**, and **Paste** commands to move or copy slides in the presentation. Follow these steps:

1. Change to Slide Sorter view, or display Normal view and work with the Outline or Slides panes.

2. Select the slide(s) you want to copy or cut.

3 Open the **Edit** menu and select **Cut** or **Copy** to either move or copy the slide(s), respectively, or you can use the **Cut** or **Copy** toolbar buttons.

> ### Timesaver tip
>
> **Quick Cut or Copy**   From the keyboard, press **Ctrl+C** to copy or **Ctrl+X** to cut.

4 In Slide Sorter view, select the slide after which you want to place the cut or copied slide(s), or on the Outline pane, move the insertion point to the end of the text in the slide after which you want to insert the cut or copied slide(s).

5 Select the **Edit** menu and choose **Paste**, or click the **Paste** toolbar button. PowerPoint inserts the cut or copied slides.

> ### Timesaver tip
>
> **Keyboard Shortcut**   You can also press **Ctrl+V** to paste an item that you cut or copied.

6 Rearranging Slides in a Presentation

In this lesson, you learn how to rearrange your slides using the Slide Sorter view and the Outline/Slides pane.

→ Rearranging Slides in Slide Sorter View

Slide Sorter view shows thumbnails of the slides in your presentation. This enables you to view many if not all slides in the presentation at one time. Slide Sorter view provides the ideal environment for arranging slides in the appropriate order for your presentation. To rearrange slides in Slide Sorter view, perform the following steps:

1 If necessary, switch to Slide Sorter view by selecting **View** and then choosing **Slide Sorter**.

2 Place the mouse pointer on the slide you want to move.

3 Hold down the left mouse button and drag the slide to a new position in the presentation. The mouse pointer becomes a small slide box.

4 To position the slide, place the mouse before or after another slide in the presentation. A vertical line appears before or after the slide (see Figure 6.1).

> **Important**
>
> **Destination Not in View?** If you have more than just a few slides in your presentation, you might not be able to see the slide's final destination in the Slide Sorter. Don't worry; just drag the slide in the direction of the destination, and the Slide Sorter pane scrolls in that direction.

5 Release the mouse button. PowerPoint places the slide into its new position and shifts the surrounding slides to make room for the inserted slide.

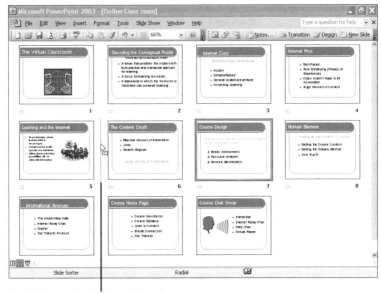

Vertical line indicates the slide's placement

Figure 6.1 **Drag a slide in the presentation to a new position.**

You can also copy a slide in Slide Sorter view as easily as you can move a slide. Simply hold down the **Ctrl** key while you drag the slide. When you release the mouse, PowerPoint inserts a copy of the selected slide into the presentation.

Although the Slides pane on the left side of the Normal view window does not provide as much workspace as the Slide Sorter, you can use the techniques discussed in this section to move or copy a slide. The Slides pane probably works best when you have only a few slides in the presentation. When you have a large number of slides, you might want to switch from the Normal view to the Slide Sorter view.

→ Rearranging Slides in the Outline Pane

In the Outline pane of the Normal view, you see the presentation as an outline that numbers each slide and shows its title and slide text. This provides you with a pretty good picture of the content and overall organization of your presentation. To rearrange the slides in your presentation using the Outline pane, follow these steps:

1. Switch to the Normal view by selecting **View**, **Normal**, or by clicking the **Normal** button on the bottom left of the PowerPoint window.

2. Click the slide number you want to move. This highlights the contents of the entire slide.

3. Place the mouse on the slide icon for that particular slide and drag the slide up or down within the presentation; then release the mouse.

Timesaver tip

Use the Up or Down Buttons   You can also move a slide in the outline by selecting the slide and then using the **Move Up** or **Move Down** buttons on the Outlining toolbar.

→ Hiding Slides

Before you give a presentation, you should try to anticipate any questions that your audience might have and be prepared to answer those questions. You might even want to create slides to support your answers to these questions and then keep the slides hidden until you need them. To hide one or more slides, perform the following steps:

1. In the Slide Sorter view or the Slides pane of the Normal view, select the slides you want to hide.

2. Select the **Slide Show** menu and then select **Hide Slide**. In the Slide Sorter view and in the Slides pane, the hidden slide's number appears in a box with a line through it (see Figure 6.2).

3. To unhide the slides, display or select the hidden slides, choose the **Slide Show** menu, and then select **Hide Slide** (the Hide Slide command toggles the slides from hidden to unhidden).

Remember that the slides are only hidden when you actually show the presentation. You can still edit or otherwise manipulate the slides in PowerPoint (in the other views, such as Normal view) even if you have marked them as "hidden."

Hidden slides

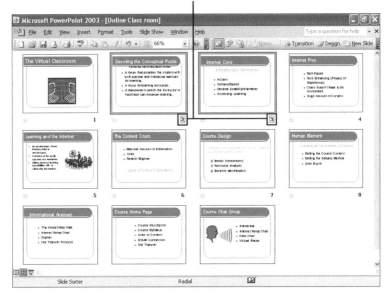

Figure 6.2 Hidden slides are denoted by a line through the slide number (slides 2 and 3 in this figure).

Timesaver tip

Right-Click Shortcut   To quickly hide a slide, you can right-click it and ooloot **Hido Slide** from the shortcut menu that appears. To unhide the slide, right-click it again and select **Hide Slide** again.

7 Adding and Modifying Slide Text

In this lesson, you learn how to add text boxes to a slide and change the text alignment and line spacing.

→ Creating a Text Box

As you learned in Lesson 3, "Working with Slides in Different Views," the text on slides resides in various text boxes. To edit the text in a text box, click in the box to place the insertion point, and then enter or edit the text within the box. If you want to add additional text to a slide that will not be contained in one of the text boxes already on the slide, you must create a new text box.

> **Jargon buster**
>
> **Text Box** A text box acts as a receptacle for the text. Text boxes often contain bulleted lists, notes, and labels (used to point to important parts of illustrations).

To create a text box, perform the following steps:

1. If necessary, switch to the Normal view (select **View**, **Normal**). Use the Slides or Outline tab on the left of the workspace to select the slide that you want to work on. The slide appears in the Slide pane.

2. Click the **Text Box** button on the Drawing toolbar (if the Drawing toolbar isn't visible, right-click any toolbar and select **Drawing**).

3. Click the slide where you want the text box to appear. A small text box appears (see Figure 7.1). (It will expand as you type in it.)

4. Type the text that you want to appear in the text box. Press **Enter** to start a new paragraph. Don't worry if the text box becomes too wide; you can resize it after you are done typing.

5 When you are finished, click anywhere outside the text box to see how the text appears on the finished slide.

Inserted text box

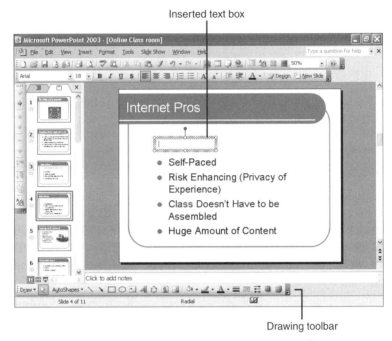

Drawing toolbar

Figure 7.1 **Text boxes can be inserted from the Drawing toolbar.**

If the text does not align correctly in the text box, see the section "Changing the Text Alignment and Line Spacing" later in this lesson to learn how to change it.

You can also add a text box via the Insert menu. Select **Insert**, then **Textbox**. Then use the mouse to "draw" the text box on the slide. Using this command set to create a textbox actually allows you to create the width of the text box before you enter the text.

Sizing and Moving Text Boxes

You can size any of the text boxes on a slide. You can also move them on the slide. To size a text box follow these steps:

1 Select the text box.

2 Place the mouse on any of the sizing handles that appear on the box (they will be small round circles).

3 When you place the mouse on the sizing handle a sizing tool appears. Click and drag the sizing handle to change the size of the box. To retain the height-width ratio of the text box, use a sizing handle on any of the text box corners and drag on the diagonal. To move a text box, place the mouse pointer on any of the box borders. The mouse pointer becomes a move tool. Drag the box to any location on the slide.

Timesaver tip

Rotate a Text Box   You can rotate a text box using the green rotation handle that appears at the top center of a selected text box. Place the mouse pointer on the handle, and the rotation icon appears. Use the mouse to drag the rotation handle to the desired position to rotate the box.

7

Deleting a Text Box

You can delete text boxes from your slides. Select the text box (so that handles appear around it and no insertion point appears inside it), and then press the **Delete** key.

If you want to delete multiple text boxes, select the first text box and then select other text boxes with the mouse while holding down the **Ctrl** key. This will select each additional text box. Press the **Delete** key to delete the text boxes.

→ Changing Font Attributes

You can enhance your text by using the Font dialog box or by using various tools on the Formatting toolbar. Use the Font dialog box if you want to add several enhancements to your text at one time. Use the Formatting toolbar to add one font enhancement at a time.

Jargon buster

Fonts, Styles, and Effects   In PowerPoint, a font is a family of text that has the same design or typeface (for example, Arial or Courier). A style is a standard enhancement, such as bold or italic. An effect is a special enhancement, such as shadow or underline.

Using the Font Dialog Box

The font dialog box offers you control over all the attributes you can apply to text. Attributes such as strikethrough, superscript, subscript, and shadow are available as check boxes in this dialog box.

You can change the font of existing text or of text you are about to type by performing the following steps:

1 To change the font of existing text, select text by clicking and dragging the I-beam pointer over the text in a particular text box. If you want to change font attributes for all the text in a text box, select the text box (do not place the insertion point within the text box).

2 Choose the **Format** menu and then choose **Font**. The Font dialog box appears, as shown in Figure 7.2.

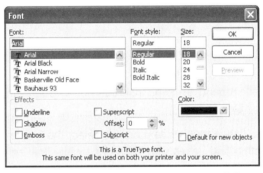

Figure 7.2 The Font dialog box enables you to change all the text attributes for selected text.

Timesaver tip

Right-Click Shortcut   You can right-click the text and select **Font** from the shortcut menu to open the Font dialog box.

3 From the **Font** list, select the font you want to use.

4 From the Font Style list, select any style you want to apply to the text, such as **Bold** or **Italic**. (To remove styles from text, select **Regular**.)

5 From the Size list, select any size in the list, or type a size directly into the box. (With TrueType fonts—the fonts marked with the TT logo—you can type any point size, even sizes that do not appear on the list.)

6 In the Effects box, select any special effects you want to add to the text, such as **Underline**, **Shadow**, or **Emboss**. You can also choose **Superscript** or **Subscript**, although these are less common.

7 To change the color of your text, click the arrow button to the right of the Color list and click the desired color. (For more colors, click the **More Colors** option at the bottom of the Color drop-down list; to select a color, use the dialog box that appears.)

8 Click **OK** to apply the new look to your selected text.

> **Timesaver tip**
>
> **Title and Object Area Text** If you change a font on an individual slide, the font change applies only to that slide. To change the font for all the slides in the presentation, you need to change the font on the Slide Master. Select **View**, point at **Master**, and then select **Slide Master**. Select a text area and perform the preceding steps to change the look of the text on all slides. Be careful, however, because these changes override any font styles that are supplied by the design template assigned to the presentation.

Formatting Text with the Formatting Toolbar

The Formatting toolbar provides several buttons that enable you to change font attributes for the text on your slides. It makes it easy for you to quickly bold selected text or to change the color of text in a text box.

To use the different Formatting toolbar font tools, follow these steps:

1 To change the look of existing text, select the text, or select a particular text box to change the look of all the text within that box.

2 To change fonts, open the **Font** drop-down list and click the desired font.

3 To change font size, open the **Font Size** drop-down list, click the desired size or type a size directly into the box, and then press **Enter**.

> **Timesaver tip**
>
> **Incrementing the Type Size** To increase or decrease the text size to the next size up or down, click the Increase Font Size or Decrease Font Size buttons on the Formatting toolbar.

4 To add a style or effect to the text (bold, italic, underline, and/or shadow), click the appropriate button(s):

B Bold

I Italic

U Underline

S Shadow

As you have already seen, you can change the font color through the Font dialog box. You can also change it with the Font Color button on the Formatting toolbar. Just do the following:

1. Select the text for which you want to change the color.

2 Click the down-pointing arrow next to the **Font Color** button on the Formatting toolbar. A color palette appears (see Figure 7.3).

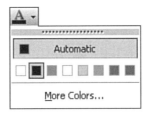

Figure 7.3 When you click the arrow next to the Font Colors button, a color palette appears.

3 Do one of the following:

▪ Click a color on the palette to change the color of the selected text or the text box (the colors available are based on the design template and color scheme you have selected for the presentation).

▪ Click the **More Font Colors** option to display a Colors dialog box. Click a color on the Standard tab or use the Custom tab to create your own color. Then click **OK**. The color is applied to the text.

→ Copying Text Formats

If your presentation contains text with a format you want to use, you can copy that text's format and apply it to other text on the slide (or other slides). To copy text formats, perform the following steps:

1 Highlight the text with the format you want to use.

2 Click the **Format Painter** button on the toolbar. PowerPoint copies the format.

3 Drag the mouse pointer (which now looks like the Format Painter icon) across the text to which you want to apply the format.

If you want to apply a format to different text lines or even different text boxes on a slide or slides, double-click the Format Painter button. Use the mouse to apply styles to as many text items as you want. Then, click the Format Painter button again to turn off the feature.

→ Changing the Text Alignment and Line Spacing

When you first type text, PowerPoint automatically places it against the left edge of the text box. To change the paragraph alignment, perform the following steps:

1 Click anywhere inside the paragraph you want to realign (a paragraph is any text line or wrapped text lines followed by a line break—created when you press the **Enter** key).

2 Select the **Format** menu and then select **Alignment**. The Alignment submenu appears (see Figure 7.4).

3 Select **Align Left**, **Center**, **Align Right**, or **Justify** to align the paragraph as required.

Timesaver tip

    Some Alignment Shortcuts To quickly set left alignment, press **Ctrl+L** or click the **Align Left** button on the Formatting toolbar. For centered alignment, press **Ctrl+C** or click the **Center** button. For right alignment, press **Ctrl+R** or click the **Align Right** button.

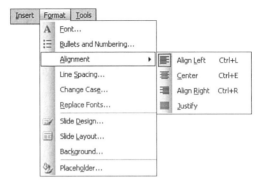

Figure 7.4 You can align each text line or paragraph in a text box.

If you want to align all the text in a text box in the same way (rather than aligning the text line by line), select the entire text box (click the box border) and then use the Alignment menu selection or the alignment buttons on the Formatting toolbar.

You can also change the spacing between text lines (remember, PowerPoint considers these to be paragraphs) in a text box. The default setting for line spacing is single space. To change the line spacing in a paragraph, perform these steps:

1. Click inside the paragraph you want to change, or select all the paragraphs you want to change by selecting the entire text box.

2. Select **Format**, **Line Spacing**. The Line Spacing dialog box appears, as shown in Figure 7.5

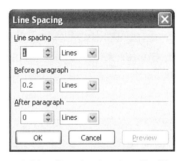

Figure 7.5 Select Format, Line Spacing to open the Line Spacing dialog box.

3. Click the arrow buttons to the right of any of the following text boxes to change the spacing for the following:

- Line Spacing—This setting controls the space between the lines in a paragraph.

- Before Paragraph—This setting controls the space between this paragraph and the paragraph that comes before it.

- After Paragraph—This setting controls the space between this paragraph and the paragraph that comes after it.

4 After you make your selections, click **OK**.

Timesaver tip

Lines or Points? The drop-down list box that appears to the right of each setting enables you to set the line spacing in lines or points. A line is the current line height (based on the current text size). A point is a unit commonly used to measure text. One point is 1/72 of an inch.

→ Adding a WordArt Object

PowerPoint comes with an add-on program called WordArt (which is also available in other Office applications, such as Word and Excel) that can help you create graphical text effects. You can create text wrapped in a circle and text that has 3D effects and other special alignment options. To insert a WordArt object onto a slide, perform the following steps:

1 In the Slide view, display the slide on which you want to place the WordArt object.

2 Click the **Insert** menu, point at **Picture**, and then select **WordArt** (or select the WordArt button on the Drawing toolbar). The WordArt Gallery dialog box appears, showing many samples of WordArt types.

3 Click the sample that best represents the WordArt type you want and click **OK**. The Edit WordArt Text dialog box appears (see Figure 7.6).

4 Choose a font and size from the respective drop-down lists.

5 Type the text you want to use into the Text box.

6 Click **OK**. PowerPoint creates the WordArt text on your slide, as shown in Figure 7.7.

Figure 7.6 Enter the text, size, and font to be used into the Edit WordArt Text dialog box.

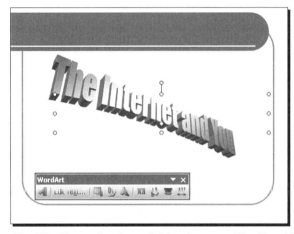

Figure 7.7 The WordArt toolbar is available when your WordArt object is selected.

After you have created WordArt, you have access to the WordArt toolbar, shown in Figure 7.7. You can use it to modify your WordArt. Table 7.1 summarizes the toolbar's buttons.

Table 7.1 **Buttons on the WordArt Toolbar**

To Do This	Click This
Insert a new WordArt object	
Edit the text, size, and font of the selected WordArt object	Edit Text...
Change the style of the current WordArt object in the WordArt Gallery	
Open a Format WordArt dialog box	
Change the shape of the WordArt	
Make all the letters the same height	
Toggle between vertical and horizontal text orientation	
Change the text alignment	
Change the spacing between letters	

You can rotate a WordArt object by dragging the rotation handle on the WordArt box. To edit the WordArt object, double-click it to display the WordArt toolbar and text entry box. Enter your changes and then click outside the WordArt object. You can move the object by dragging its border or resize it by dragging a handle.

8 Creating Columns, Tables, and Lists

In this lesson, you learn how to use tabs to create columns of text, bulleted lists, numbered lists, and other types of lists.

→ Working in Multiple Columns

Depending on the type of slide that you are creating, you might need to arrange text on a slide in multiple columns. PowerPoint provides three options for placing text into columns on a slide:

- You can use the Title and 2 Column slide layout to create a slide with side-by-side text columns.
- You can place tab stops in a single text box and press **Tab** to create columns for your text.
- You can use a table to create a two- or multiple-column text grid.

In this lesson, you learn about all these methods.

Creating Columns with a Slide Layout

The easiest way to create columns of text is to change a slide's layout so that it provides side-by-side text boxes. Because the default layout for slides is a slide with a title box and a single text box, you will probably need to use the Slide Layout task pane to change its format to include two text columns. Follow these steps:

1. Create a new slide or select a slide that you want to format with the two-column layout (using the Outline or Slides pane).
2. Open the task pane (select **View**, **Task Pane**).
3. Select the task pane drop-down arrow and select **Slide Layout**.
4. Click the **Title and 2 Column** slide layout from the Text Layouts section of the Slide Layout task pane to format the slide (see Figure 8.1).

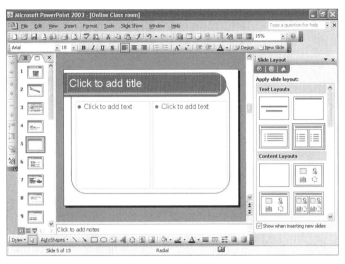

Figure 8.1 **A two-column slide layout provides two panes in which to enter text.**

You can then type the text that you want to appear in the two text boxes provided on the slide.

Timesaver tip

Position the Cursor on a Slide Layout to See Its Description   If you position the cursor on any of the slide layouts in the Slide Layout task pane, a tip appears, describing the layout.

Using Tabs to Create Columns

You can also create multiple columns in a text box using tab stops. To set the tabs for a multicolumn list, perform the following steps:

1. Open the presentation and select the slide you want to work with in Slide view.

2. Make sure that the ruler is showing in the PowerPoint window (select **View**, then **Ruler** if necessary).

3. Select **Insert**, then **Textbox**. Drag the mouse to create a textbox that is as wide as the area on the ruler that you will use to set the tabs. The ruler area will display the usable area on the slide (white) and the margins on the slide (dark gray). If you do not see the ruler, select the **View** menu and then select **Ruler** to display the ruler.

4 Click anywhere inside the text box. After the insertion point is in the text box, you can set the tabs.

5 If you already typed text inside the text box, select the text.

6 Click the **Tab** button at the left end of the ruler until it represents the type of tab you want to set (see Table 8.1 for more information on the type of tabs available).

7 Click in various positions on the ruler to place a tab stop using the type of tab you currently have selected. Figure 8.2 shows several tab stops that have been placed in a text box.

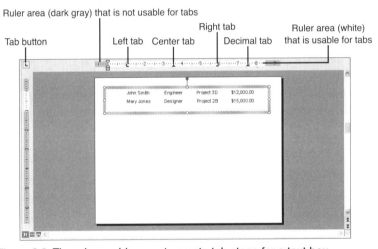

Figure 8.2 The ruler enables you to create tab stops for a text box.

8 Repeat steps 6 and 7 if you want to set different types of tab stops at different positions.

9 To change the position of an existing tab stop setting, drag it on the ruler to the desired position. To delete an existing tab stop setting, drag it off the ruler.

10 (Optional) To hide the ruler, select the **View** menu and then select **Ruler**.

Table 8.1 Tab Button Stop Types

Button Appearance	Tab Stop Type
	Aligns the left end of the line against the tab stop.
	Centers the text on the tab stop.
	Aligns the right end of the line against the tab stop.
	Aligns the tab stop on a period. This is called a decimal tab and Is useful for aligning a column of numbers that uses decimal points.

Creating a Table

Tables can also be used to place text in side-by-side columns. You can create tables that provide two columns, three columns, or any number of columns that you require. Tables are also very useful when you want to display numerical information in a grid layout or information that you want to arrange in rows. A table is a collection of intersecting columns and rows. The block created when a column and a row intersects is often referred to as a *cell*. The easiest way to create a table on a slide is to use the Table layout. Follow these steps:

1. Create a new slide or select a slide that you want to format with the Table layout (using the Outline or Slides pane).

2. Open the task pane (select **View**, **Task Pane**).

3. Select the task pane drop-down arrow and select **Slide Layout**.

4. Scroll down through layouts in the task pane, and then click the **Title and Table** layout. This assigns the Title and Table layout to the current slide (see Figure 8.3).

5. After you assign the Title and Table layout to the slide, you can set the number of columns and rows for the table. Double-click the Table icon on the slide. The Insert dialog box appears.

6. Specify the number of columns and rows that you want in the table and then click **OK**. The table is placed on the slide.

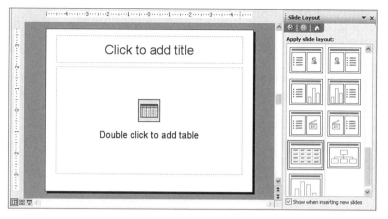

Figure 8.3 The Table layout enables you to place a table on a slide.

You can also insert a table onto an existing slide. This allows you to include a table on a slide where you don't want to change the slide's layout as discussed in the preceding steps. Follow these steps:

1. Display the slide on which you want to place the table.

2. Select the **Insert** menu and then choose **Table**. The Insert Table dialog box appears.

3. Enter the number of columns and rows that you want to have in the table.

4. Click **OK**. The table appears on the slide.

When the table appears on the slide, the Tables and Borders toolbar also appears in the PowerPoint window (we will use this toolbar in a moment). After you have a table on a slide, you can work with it like this:

- Click inside a table cell and enter your text. You can move from cell to cell by pressing **Tab** to go forward or **Shift+Tab** to go back. Enter text as needed.

- If you need to resize the table, drag a selection handle, the same as you would any object.

- To adjust the row height or column width, position the mouse pointer on a line between two rows or columns and drag. The mouse pointer becomes a sizing tool when you place it on any column or row border.

- If you want to change the style of the borders around certain cells on the table (or the entire table), select the cells (drag the mouse across the cells to select them). You can then use the buttons on the Tables and Borders toolbar to change the border attributes (see Figure 8.4). Use the Border Style button and the Border Width button to change the border style and border line weight, respectively. If you want to change the border color, use the Border Color button. Use the buttons on the Tables and Borders toolbar to adjust the thickness and style of the table gridlines.

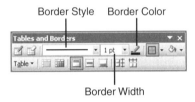

Figure 8.4 Border attributes for the table can be changed using the buttons on the Tables and Borders toolbar.

To make a table appear to be multiple columns of text without the table borders, turn off all the gridlines in the table. To do so, select all the cells in the table; then right-click and choose **Borders and Fill**. In the Format Table dialog box that appears (see Figure 8.5), click each of the border buttons provided on the table diagram to turn the border off for each side of each cell in the table. Click **OK** to return to the table.

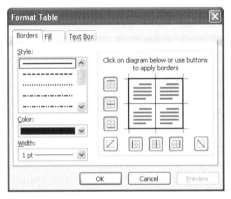

Figure 8.5 The Format Table dialog box can be used to control border lines and other table attributes.

When you enter new slides into a presentation, the default layout provides a title box and a text box that is set up as a simple bulleted list. Therefore, just creating a new slide creates a bulleted list.

You can turn off the bullets in front of any paragraphs by selecting the paragraphs and clicking the **Bullets** button on the Formatting toolbar to toggle the bullets off. If you want to remove the bullets from all the paragraphs (remember a text line followed by the Enter key is a paragraph), select the entire text box and click the **Bullets** button.

When you insert your own text boxes using the Text Box button on the Drawing toolbar, the text does not have bullets by default. You can add your own bullets by following these steps:

1 Click the text line (paragraph) that you want to format for bullets. If you want to add bullets to all the text lines in a text box, select the text box.

2 Select the **Format** menu, and then select **Bullets and Numbering**. The Bullets and Numbering dialog box appears (see Figure 8.6).

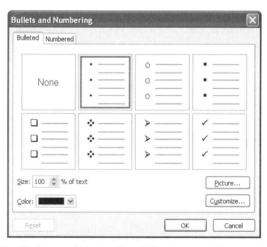

Figure 8.6 The Bullets and Numbering dialog box enables you to select the bullets for your bulleted items.

3 Select the bullet style you want to use from the list PowerPoint provides.

4 Click **OK**. PowerPoint formats the selected text into a bulleted list. (If you press **Enter** at the end of a bulleted paragraph, the next paragraph starts with a bullet.)

→ Working with Numbered Lists

Numbered lists are like bulleted lists, except they have sequential numbers instead of symbols. You can convert any paragraphs to a numbered list by selecting them and clicking the **Numbering** button on the Formatting toolbar. Select the paragraphs again and click the **Numbering** button again to toggle the numbering off.

You can also create numbered lists with the Bullets and Numbering dialog box, the same as you did with bullets. Follow these steps:

1 Select the paragraphs that you want to convert to a numbered list.

2 Choose **Format**, and then select **Bullets and Numbering**.

3 Click the **Numbered** tab on the dialog box. The numbered list styles appear (see Figure 8.7).

4 Click the number style you want for your list.

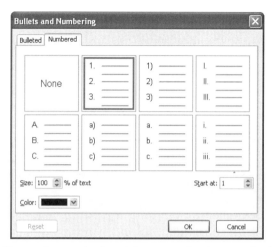

Figure 8.7 Choose the numbering style you want or turn numbering off by choosing None.

5 (Optional) Change the Size and/or Color of the numbers.

6 (Optional) If you want the list to start at a number other than 1, enter it into the **Start At** text box.

7 Click **OK**.

9 Adding Graphics to a Slide

In this lesson, you learn how to add PowerPoint clip art to your presentations and how to add images from other sources.

→ Using the Clip Art Task Pane

The Clip Art task pane provides you access to all the clip art provided with Microsoft Office. It also includes a search engine that you can use to search for clip art, photographs, movies, and sounds that are stored on your computer. You can also search for clip art and other items using Microsoft's online clip library. (You must be connected to the Internet when using PowerPoint to access the Microsoft online library.)

Figure 9.1 shows the Clip Art task pane. You can use this task pane to search for and insert images onto your slides, or you can take advantage of slides that use a layout that contains a placeholder for images and clip art.

You learn about using the Clip Art task pane and slide layouts that provide image placeholders in this lesson. In Lesson 10, "Adding Sounds and Movies to a Slide," you take a look at using the Clip Art task pane to add movies and slides to your PowerPoint slides.

Jargon buster

Clip Art A collection of previously created images or pictures that you can place on a slide. Microsoft Office provides clip art and other media types, such as movies and sounds.

You can open the Clip Art task pane in any of these ways:

- Click the **Insert Clip Art** button on the Drawing toolbar.
- Select the **Insert** menu, point at **Picture**, and then choose **Clip Art**.

- Open the task pane, click the task pane drop-down arrow, and then select **Insert Clip Art** to switch to the Clip Art task pane.

Figure 9.1 The Clip Art task pane manages pictures, motion clips, and sounds—all in one convenient place.

When you use the Clip Art task pane, you search for images by keywords. In the following sections, you take a look at inserting clip art from the task pane and learn how you can insert clip art using some of the slide layouts (that provide a clip art placeholder on the slide).

Timesaver tip

Clip Organizer Scan The first time you open the Clip Art task pane, PowerPoint prompts you to allow the Clip Organizer (which is discussed later in the lesson) to search your hard drive. Clip Organizer then creates category folders and image indexes from the clip art and images that it finds there. Click **Yes** to allow this process to take place.

→ Inserting an Image from the Task Pane

As previously mentioned, the Clip Art task pane allows you to search for clip art files using keywords. If you wanted to search for clip art of cats, you would search for the word "cats." To insert a piece of the clip art using the task pane, follow these steps:

1 Select the slide on which you want to place the image so that it appears in the Slide pane.

2 Select **Insert**, point at **Picture**, and then select **Clip Art**. The Clip Art task pane appears.

3 Type keywords into the Search Text box in the task pane that will be used to find your clip art images.

4 Click the **Search** button. Images that match your search criteria appear in the task pane as thumbnails.

5 In the Results list, locate the image that you want to place on the slide. Then click the image, and the clip art is placed on the slide (see Figure 9.2).

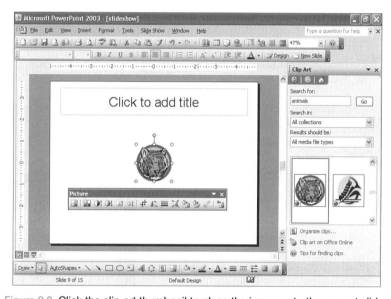

Figure 9.2 Click the clip art thumbnail to place the image onto the current slide.

You can use the sizing handles on the image to size the clip art box. Or you can drag the clip art box to a new location on the slide.

→ Inserting an Image from an Image Box

Another way that you can add clip art images to a slide in your presentation is to create the slide using a slide format that supplies a clip art placeholder box on the slide. These slide layout types are called content layouts because they make it easy to insert objects such as clip art, charts, and other items onto a slide. You can then use the object placeholder on the slide to access the clip art library and insert a particular image onto the slide.

Follow these steps:

1 Create a new slide or select the slide you want to assign a layout to that contains a clip art placeholder box.

2 Open the task pane (**View**, **Task Pane**) and then click the task pane drop-down menu and select **Slide Layout** (the Slide Layout task pane automatically opens if you've just created a new slide).

3 Scroll down through the layouts provided until you locate either the Content layout or the Text and Content layout. Both of these layout categories provide slide layouts that contain object placeholders or object placeholders and text boxes, respectively.

4 Select the layout that best suits the purpose of your slide (see Figure 9.3).

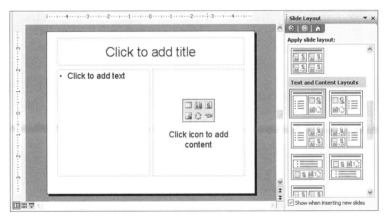

Figure 9.3 **Select a slide layout that contains an object placeholder.**

5 The slide layout you choose provides you with a placeholder box that contains icons for tables, charts, clip art, and other objects. Click the **Insert Clip Art** icon in the placeholder box. The Select Picture dialog box appears (see Figure 9.4).

6 Scroll down through the list of clip art and other images to find a particular image (the list will be lengthy because it includes all the Office Clip Art and any other images that were located on your computer when the Clip Organizer cataloged the images on your computer).

7 If you want, you can search for particular images by keyword. Type the search criteria into the Search Text box and then click **Search**. Images that match the search criteria appear in the Select Picture dialog box.

8 Click the picture thumbnail that you want to place on the slide. Then click **OK**.

Figure 9.4 The Select Picture dialog box enables you to scroll through or search through the entire clip art and image library on your computer.

PowerPoint places the image on the slide in the object placeholder box. You can size the box or move it on the slide.

→ Inserting a Clip from a File

If you have an image stored on your computer that you would like to place on a slide, you can insert the picture directly from the file. This means that you don't have to use the Clip Art task pane to search for and then insert the image.

To place a graphical image on a slide directly from a file, follow these steps:

1 Select the slide on which the image will be placed.

2 Select the **Insert** menu, point at **Picture**, and then select **From File**. The Insert Picture dialog box appears (see Figure 9.5).

3 Select the picture you want to use. You can view all the picture files in a particular location as thumbnails. Select the **Views** button, and then select **Thumbnails** on the menu that appears.

4 Click **Insert** to place the image on the slide.

If the picture is too big or too small, you can drag the selection handles (the small squares) around the edge of the image to resize it. Hold down the **Shift** key to proportionally resize the image (this maintains the height/width ratio of the image so that you cannot stretch or distort it). See Lesson 11, "Working with PowerPoint Objects," for more details about resizing and cropping images and other objects on a slide.

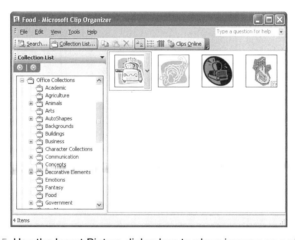

Figure 9.5 Use the Insert Picture dialog box to place images on a slide.

Timesaver tip

Link It Up   You can link a graphic to the presentation so that whenever the original changes, the version in the presentation changes, too. Just open the drop-down list on the Insert button in the Insert Picture dialog box (refer to Figure 9.5) and choose **Link to File**.

→ Managing Images in the Clip Organizer

Occasionally, you might want to add or delete clip art images from folders on your computer. Managing images is accomplished using the Clip Organizer. When you install Microsoft Office 2003 (using the default installation), a fairly large library of clip art is placed on your hard drive in different category folders. You can manage these clip art images and other images on your computer, such as scanned images or pictures from a digital camera. To open the Clip Organizer, follow these steps:

1 With the Clip Art task pane open in the PowerPoint window, click the **Clip Organizer** link near the bottom of the task pane to open the Clip Organizer.

2 (Optional) The first time you open the Organizer, you will be given the opportunity to catalog all the media files (clip art, photos, videos) on your computer. Click the **Now** button to catalog all media.

3 To view the clip art categories Microsoft Office has provided, click the plus sign (+) to the left of the Office Collections folder in the Collection list (this folder is located on the left side of the Clip Organizer window). Category folders such as Academic, Agriculture, and so on will appear in the Collection list.

4 Click one of the category folders to view the clip art that it holds (for example, click **Food**). The clip art in that category folder appears in the Clip Organizer window (see Figure 9.6).

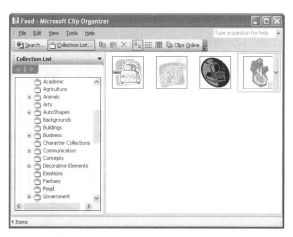

Figure 9.6 Use the Clip Organizer to manage your clip art and image files.

Not only does the Clip Organizer allow you to browse the various clip art and other images on your computer, it allows you to copy, delete, or move images. For example, if you find an image you no longer want to store on your computer, select the image in the Clip Organizer window and press **Delete**. A dialog box appears, letting you know that this image will be removed from all collections on the computer. Click **OK** to delete the image.

You can also use the Clip Organizer to copy or move clip art images from a location on your hard drive to one of the clip art collections. Locate the images you want to move or copy to a particular collection and then select them.

To move the images to a collection, select the **Edit** menu, and then **Move to Collection**. The Move to Collection dialog box appears (see Figure 9.7). Select a location in the dialog box and click **OK** to move the selected image or images.

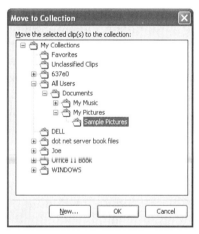

Figure 9.7 **You can move images from one location to another using the Clip Organizer.**

You can also copy images to a new location using the Copy to Collection command. Select the images in a particular folder on your computer using the Clip Organizer window. Select the **Edit** menu and then **Copy to Collection**. Select a location in the Copy to Collection dialog box where you would like to place copies of the images, and then click **OK**.

10 Adding Sounds and Movies to a Slide

In this lesson, you learn how to add sound and video clips to a PowerPoint presentation.

→ Working with Sounds and Movies

A great way to add some interest to your PowerPoint presentations is to add sounds and movies to your slides. Sounds enable you to emphasize certain slides, and movie animations can add humor and style to your presentations. Next, you take a look at adding sounds and then adding movie animations to your slides.

> **Important**
>
> **Too Much Media Can Be Distracting** Too many sounds, movies, and even images can be distracting to your audience and clutter your slides. Use sounds, movies, and images to add interest, not confusion.

→ Including Sounds in a Presentation

Sounds can be used to add emphasis to information on slides or to add some auditory interest to your presentation. You can place sound files on your slides in two different ways:

- You can insert a sound clip as an icon on a slide. When you click the icon, the sound plays.
- You can assign a sound to another object on a slide so that when you click the object, the sound plays. For example, you could assign a sound to an image. When you click the image, the sound plays (sounds added to PowerPoint animations play when the animation plays).

Inserting a Sound onto a Slide

To insert a sound clip as an object onto a slide, you can either use the Clip Art task pane or insert the sound as a file. The Clip Art task pane can provide you only with sound files that have been included in the Office clip art library or sound files that you have added to your collection using the Clip Organizer (which is discussed in the previous lesson). Any sound file that you have recorded or otherwise acquired can be inserted as a file.

To insert a sound clip from the Clip Art task pane, follow these steps:

1 Select the slide on which you will place the sound, so that it appears in the Slide pane.

2 Select **Insert**, point at **Movies and Sounds**, and then select **Sound from Clip Organizer**. The Clip Art task pane appears with a list of sound files. You can use the Search For box to search for a particular type of sound file by keyword.

3 To preview a particular sound file, point at the file and click the menu arrow that appears. Select **Preview/Properties** from the menu. The Preview/Properties dialog box for that sound file appears (see Figure 10.1).

Figure 10.1 **Preview a sound clip before placing it onto a slide.**

4 The sound will play automatically when the Preview/Properties dialog box opens. You can click the **Stop**, **Pause**, or **Play** buttons in the dialog box to perform that particular function. When you have finished previewing a sound file, click **Close** to close the Preview/Properties dialog box.

5 When you are ready to insert a sound file onto the slide, click the sound file on the task pane.

6 A dialog box opens, asking you whether you want the sound to play automatically when you run the slide show. Click **Yes** to have the sound played automatically. Click **No** to set up the sound so that you will have to click it during the slide show to play the sound.

Regardless of whether you choose to have PowerPoint play the sound automatically, it appears as a sound icon on the slide.

If you have recorded a sound file or have acquired a sound file that you want to use on a slide without using the Clip Art task pane, you can insert it as a file. To insert a sound clip from a file, follow these steps:

1 Choose the **Insert** menu, point at **Movies and Sounds**, and then choose **Sound from File**.

2 In the Insert Sound dialog box, navigate to the drive and folder containing the sound you want to use (see Figure 10.2).

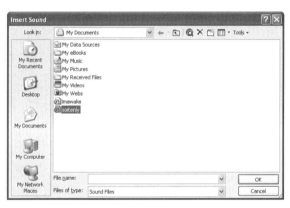

Figure 10.2 Choose the sound clip you want to include on your slide.

3 Select the sound clip and then click **OK**.

4 A dialog box opens, asking you whether you want the sound to play automatically when you run the slide show or play when you click on the sound icon on the slide. Click **Automatically** to have the sound played automatically or **When Clicked** to set up the sound so that you will have to click it during the slide show to play the sound.

The sound file appears on the slide as a sound icon. If you want to play the sound file on the slide, right-click the sound icon and select **Play Sound** from the shortcut menu.

Associating a Sound with Another Object on the Slide

If you want to avoid having a sound icon on your slide, you can associate the sound with some other object already on the slide, such as a graphic. To do so, follow these steps:

1 Right-click the object (such as a clip art image) to which you want to assign the sound.

2 Choose **Action Settings** from the shortcut menu. The Actions Settings dialog box appears.

3 If you want the sound to play when the object is pointed at, click the **Mouse Over** tab. Otherwise, click the **Mouse Click** tab. The Mouse Click option requires that the sound icon be clicked on for the sound to play.

4 Click the **Play Sound** check box. A drop-down list of sounds becomes available (see Figure 10.3).

Figure 10.3 Choose a sound to be associated with the object.

5 Open the **Play Sound** drop-down list and choose the sound you want.

If the sound you want is not on the list, choose **Other Sound** and locate the sound using the Add Sound dialog box that appears. Select the sound from there and click **OK**.

6 When you have chosen the sound you want, click **OK** to close the Action Settings dialog box.

Now, when you are giving the presentation, you can play the sound by either clicking or pointing at the object (depending on how you configured the sound to play). To test this, jump to the Slide Show view (select the **View** menu and then click **Slide Show**) and try it out. Press **Esc** to return to the Normal view when you are finished testing the sound file.

→ Placing a Movie onto a Slide

The procedure for placing a movie onto a slide is very much the same as that for a sound. You can place a movie using the Clip Art task pane or from a file. You will find that the task pane Clip Organizer provides several movies that can be used to add interest to your slides. To insert a movie onto a slide, follow these steps:

10

1 Choose the **Insert** menu, point at **Movies and Sounds**, and then select **Movies from Clip Organizer**. Use the Search box if you want to locate movies using a keyword search.

2 Scroll through the movies listed on the Clip Art task pane.

3 Point at a movie clip you want to preview. Click the menu arrow that appears and select **Preview/Properties**. The Preview Properties dialog box for the movie appears.

4 PowerPoint previews the movie on the left side of the dialog box (see Figure 10.4). If you want to place a caption onto the movie clip, click in the **Caption** box below the Preview pane and type a caption.

5 Click **Close** to close the Preview/Properties dialog box. To insert the movie into your slide, click the movie in the task pane.

6 A dialog box will open allowing you to choose how the movie will be started during the slide show. Click **Automatically** to start the movie automatically when the slide is shown during the slide show or **When Clicked**, which will require that you click the movie to play it during the slide show.

After the movie icon is in place on your slide, you can size the movie box using the usual sizing handles or move it to another position on the slide. If you want to test view the movie on the slide, jump to the Slide Show view (select the **View** menu and then click **Slide Show**) and try it out. Press **Esc** to return to the Normal view when you are finished testing the movie.

Timesaver tip

Clip Organizer Movies Really Aren't Movies The Clip Organizer movies provided by Microsoft Office are really just animations. They are designed to play automatically when the slide containing the image is opened during a slide show.

You can also place actual videos on a slide as a file. This enables you to place video captures that you have created or video files from other sources.

Follow these steps:

1. Choose the **Insert** menu, point at **Movies and Sounds**, and then choose **Movie from File**.
2. In the Insert Sound dialog box that appears, navigate to the drive and folder containing the movie file you want to use.
3. Select the file and click **OK** to place it on the slide.

4 A dialog box appears that enables you to have the movie play when the slide appears in the slide show. Click **Automatically**. To require that you click the movie's icon to make it play during the slide show, click **When Clicked**.

After you make your selection in step 4, PowerPoint places the movie onto the slide. To preview the video file on the slide, right-click the video icon and then select **Play Movie**.

11 | Working with PowerPoint Objects

In this lesson, you learn how to manipulate objects on your slides, such as clip art and other items, to create impressive presentations.

→ Selecting Objects

In the previous two lessons, you learned about inserting clip art, image files, sound files, and movie files onto the slides of your PowerPoint presentation. Any type of special content that you place on a slide is called an object. In addition to the object types just listed, objects could also be items from other Office applications. For example, you could create an object on a slide that is actually an Excel worksheet or chart.

After you select an object, you can do all kinds of things to it, such as copying, moving, deleting, or resizing it. The following is a review of ways you can select objects on a PowerPoint slide:

- To select a single object, click it. (If you click text, a frame appears around the text. Click the frame to select the text object.)
- To select more than one object, hold down the **Ctrl** or **Shift** key while clicking each object. Handles appear around the selected objects, as shown in Figure 11.1 (this temporarily groups the objects so that you can move them all simultaneously on the slide).
- To deselect selected objects, click anywhere outside the selected object or objects.

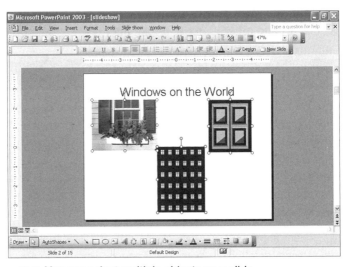

Figure 11.1 **You can select multiple objects on a slide.**

→ Working with Layers of Objects

As you place objects onscreen, they might start to overlap, creating layers of objects where the lower layers are often difficult or impossible to select. To move objects in layers, perform the following steps:

1 Click the object you want to move up or down in the stack. If the Drawing toolbar is not available in the PowerPoint window, right-click on any toolbar and select **Drawing** from the menu that appears.

2 Click the **Draw** button on the Drawing toolbar to open the Draw menu, and select **Order**, as shown in Figure 11.2.

3 Select one of the following options:

■ Bring to Front—Brings the object to the top of the stack.

■ Send to Back—Sends the object to the bottom of the stack.

- **Bring Forward**—Brings the object up one layer.
- **Send Backward**—Sends the object back one layer.

Using the different layering settings allows you to superimpose images on top of other images. For example, you could place an image of a bird on top of a picture of the sky. You can also use these settings to superimpose text on a graphic.

11

Figure 11.2 Use the Draw menu on the Drawing toolbar to change the layer on which a graphic appears on your slide.

→ Grouping and Ungrouping Objects

Each object on a slide, including text boxes, is an individual object. However, sometimes you want two or more objects to act as a group. For example, you might want to make the lines of several objects the same thickness or group several objects so that they can easily be moved together on the slide. If you want to treat two or more objects as a group, perform the following steps:

1. Select the objects you want to group. Remember, to select more than one object, hold down the **Shift** or **Ctrl** key as you click each one.

2. Click the **Draw** button on the Drawing toolbar to open the Draw menu, and then select **Group**.

3. To ungroup the objects, select any object in the group and select **Draw**, and then choose **Ungroup**.

You can cut, copy, and paste objects onto a slide (or onto another slide) the same as you would normal text. When you cut an object, PowerPoint removes the object from the slide and places it in a temporary holding area called the Office Clipboard. When you copy or cut an object, a copy of the object, or the object itself when you use Cut, is placed on the Office Clipboard. You can place multiple objects onto the Clipboard and paste them as needed onto a slide or slides in your presentation.

To view the Office Clipboard, select **View**, **Task Pane**. Then, on the task pane drop-down menu, select **Clipboard**. Figure 11.3 shows the Clipboard task pane.

Figure 11.3 **Use the Clipboard to keep track of objects that you have cut or copied.**

To cut or copy an object, perform the following steps:

 Select the object(s) you want to cut, copy, or move.

  Select the **Edit** menu and then choose **Cut** or **Copy**. Or you can use the **Cut**, **Copy**, and **Paste** buttons on the Formatting toolbar.

3   Display the slide on which you want to paste the cut or copied objects.

4   Select **Edit** and then choose **Paste**. PowerPoint pastes the objects onto the slide.

To remove an object without placing it on the Clipboard, select the object and press the **Delete** key.

→ Rotating an Object

When you select an object on a slide, a handle with a green end on it appears at the top center of the object. This is the rotation handle, and it can be used to rotate any object on a slide. The rotation handle enables you to revolve an object around a center point.

To rotate an object, do the following:

1   Click the object you want to rotate.

2   Place the mouse pointer on the object's **Rotation** handle (the green dot) until the Rotation icon appears.

3   Hold down the mouse button and drag the **Rotation** handle until the object is in the position you want.

4   Release the mouse button.

The Draw menu (on the Drawing toolbar) also enables you to rotate or flip an object. You can flip an object horizontally left or right or flip the object vertically from top to bottom. To flip an object, click the **Draw** button on the Drawing toolbar and then point at **Rotate and Flip**. Select either **Flip Horizontal** or **Flip Vertical** from the menu that appears.

Timesaver tip

Can't Find the Drawing Toolbar?   If the Drawing toolbar does not appear at the bottom of the PowerPoint application window, right-click any visible toolbar and select **Drawing**.

→ Resizing Objects

You will find that objects such as pictures and clip art are not always inserted onto a slide in the correct size. You can resize the object by performing these steps:

1 Select the object to resize. Selection handles appear.

2 Drag one of the following handles (the squares that surround the object) until the object is the desired size:

■ Drag a corner handle to change both the height and width of an object. PowerPoint retains the object's height-to-width ratio.

■ Drag a side, top, or bottom handle to change the height or width alone.

■ To keep the original center of the object stationary while sizing, hold down the **Ctrl** key while dragging a sizing handle.

3 Release the mouse button when you have completed resizing the object.

→ Cropping a Picture

In addition to resizing a picture, you can crop it; that is, you can trim a side or a corner off the picture to remove an element from the picture or cut off some whitespace. This enables you to clean up the picture within the object box.

To crop a picture, perform the following steps:

1 Click the picture you want to crop.

2 To crop the picture, you need the Picture toolbar. Right-click any toolbar currently showing in the PowerPoint window and select **Picture**. The Picture toolbar appears.

3 Click the **Crop** button on the Picture toolbar. Cropping handles appear around the picture (see Figure 11.4).

Cropping handles

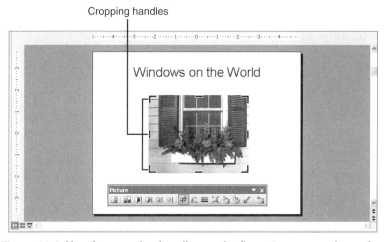

Figure 11.4 **Use the cropping handles on the figure to crop portions of the picture.**

4 Move the mouse pointer over one of the cropping handles. The mouse pointer becomes the same shape as the cropping handle. (Use a corner handle to crop two sides at once. Use a side, top, or bottom handle to crop only one side.)

5 Hold down the mouse button and drag the pointer until the crop lines are where you want them.

6 Release the mouse button. PowerPoint crops the image.

7 After cropping that image, move or resize the picture as needed.

Important

Stop That Crop!   To undo the cropping of a picture immediately after you crop it, select **Edit** and then choose **Undo Crop Picture**.

12 Presenting an Onscreen Slide Show

In this lesson, you learn how to view a slide show onscreen, how to make basic movements within a presentation, and how to set show options. You also learn how to create a self-running show with timings and how to work with slide transitions.

→ Viewing an Onscreen Slide Show

Before you show your presentation to an audience, you should run through it several times on your own computer, checking that all the slides are in the right order and that the timings and transitions between the slides work correctly. This also enables you to fine-tune any monologue you might have to give as you show the slides so that what you are saying at any point in the presentation is synchronized with the slide that is being shown at that moment.

You can preview a slide show at any time; follow these steps:

1. Open the presentation you want to view.

2. Choose the **Slide Show** menu and choose **View Show**. The first slide in the presentation appears full screen (see Figure 12.1). A series of icons appear at the bottom left of the presentation screen. There is a previous slide arrow, a pen icon, a menu icon, and a next slide arrow. We will discuss the pen and menu icons later in the lesson.

3. To display the next or the previous slide, do one of the following:

   - To display the next slide, click the left mouse button, press the **Page Down** key, or press the right-arrow or down-arrow key. You can also click the right-pointing arrow that appears at the bottom left of the slide.

   - To display the previous slide, click the right mouse button, press the **Page Up** key, or press the left-arrow or up-arrow key.

You can also click the left-pointing arrow that appears at the bottom left of the slide.

4 When you have finished running the slide show, press the **Esc** key.

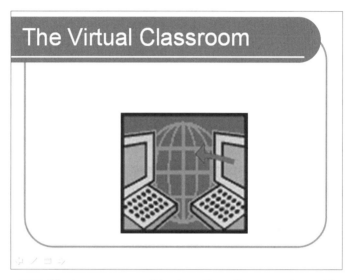

Figure 12.1 When you run your slide show, the entire screen is used to display the sides.

Timesaver tip

Start the Show! You can also start a slide show by clicking the **Slide Show** button in the bottom-left corner of the presentation window or by pressing **F5**.

→ Setting Slide Animation Schemes

After running the slide show a few times, you might find that the presentation doesn't really provide the visual impact that you had hoped. Even though you have designed your slides well and created slides that include images and movies, you are still looking for something with a more "artsy" feel. A great way to add visual impact to the presentation is to assign an animation scheme to a slide or slides in the presentation.

An animation scheme controls how the text in the text boxes on the slide appear or materialize on the slide during the presentation. For example, you can select a slide animation scheme called Bounce, where the text on the slide "bounces" onto the slide when it appears onscreen during the slide show.

Jargon buster

Animation Scheme A scheme that controls how objects materialize onto the slide during the slide show.

PowerPoint provides three categories of animation schemes that you can assign to a slide: Subtle, Moderate, and Exciting. Each of these categories provides a number of animation schemes. The great thing about the animation schemes is that you can assign them to a slide or slides and then try them out in the Normal view. If you don't like the animation scheme, you can select another.

To assign an animation scheme to a slide in the presentation, follow these steps:

1 Select the slide to which you will assign the animation scheme so that it appears in the Slide pane in the Normal view.

2 Select the **Slide Show** menu and select **Animation Schemes**. The Animation Schemes list appears in the Slide Design task pane on the right side of the PowerPoint window (see Figure 12.2).

3 Scroll through the list of animation schemes. When you find a scheme that you want to try, select the scheme in the list box.

4 To try the scheme, click the **Play** button in the task pane.

5 If you don't like the scheme, select another.

6 If you find a scheme that you would like to apply to all the slides in the presentation, click the **Apply to All Slides** button.

Timesaver tip

Assign Animation Schemes to Selected Slides You can select several slides in the Slide Sorter view and then use the Slide Design task pane to assign the same animation scheme to all the selected slides.

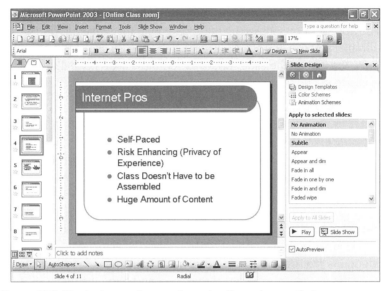

Figure 12.2 The task pane houses the animation schemes that you can assign to the slides in your presentation.

→ Setting Up a Self-Running Show

In a self-running show, the slide show runs itself. Each slide advances after a specified period of time. This allows you to concentrate on the narrative aspects of the presentation as you use the slide show for a speech or classroom presentation. For a self-running show, you must set timings. You can set the same timing for all slides (for example, a 20-second delay between each slide), or you can set a separate timing for each slide individually.

When you set up a self-running show, you can also select different slide transitions. A slide transition is a special effect that is executed when the slide appears during the slide show. For example, you can have a slide dissolve onto the screen, or you can have the slide appear on the screen using a checkerboard effect.

To configure the show to use timings and transitions, follow these steps:

1. Open the presentation you want to view.

2. Select the slide to which you would like to apply a timing or transition so that it appears in the Slides pane in the Normal view.

3 Select **Slide Show** and click **Slide Transition**. The Slide Transition task pane opens containing controls for the type of transition you want to use, the speed with which that transition executes, and the length of time the slide should remain onscreen (see Figure 12.3).

4 To select a transition for the slide, select one of the transitions supplied in the Apply to Selected Slides box.

5 To test the transition, click the **Play** button.

6 If you want to change the speed of the transition, click the Speed drop-down list and select **Slow**, **Medium**, or **Fast** (Fast is the default).

7 (Optional) If you want to select a sound to accompany the slide transition (such as Applause, Drum Roll, or Laser), click the Sound drop-down list and select one of the supplied sounds.

8 To set the timing for the slide in the Advance Slide section of the task pane, click the **Automatically After** check box. Use the click box below the check box to enter the number of seconds for the slide's automatic timing.

9 If you want to apply the selected transition and the timing to all the slides in the presentation, click the **Apply to All Slides** button.

Figure 12.3 The Slide Transition task pane houses the controls necessary for tailoring the way a slide transitions onto the screen during a presentation.

Important

My Slides Don't Advance Using the Timings   If you find when you run
the slide show that the slides don't advance using the timings that you have
set, select Slide Show, Set Up Show. In the Set Up Show dialog box, be sure
that the Using Timings, If Present option button is selected. Then click OK.

When you run the slide show, the slides advance according to the
timings that you have set. The slides also use any transitions that you
have selected for them. Take the time to run the slide show several
times so that you can gauge whether the transitions and timings work
well. Remember that the slide must be onscreen long enough for your
audience to read and understand the text on the slide.

Timesaver tip

Assign Transitions and Timings to Selected Slides   You can select
several slides in the Slide Sorter view and then use the Slide Transition task
pane to assign the same transition and/or timing to the selected slides.

Important

Don't Get Too Fancy!   If you are going to use slide transitions and
animation schemes on each and every slide, you might find that your slide
show is becoming "too exciting," like a film with too many explosions, car
chases, and other special effects. Viewers of the slide show will probably
have trouble concentrating on the text on the slides if too many things are
going on at once. Remember, everything in moderation.

→ Using the Slide Show Menu Tools

PowerPoint also provides some other features that you will find very
useful when you are running your slide show. For example, you can
turn the mouse pointer into a pen (such as a ballpoint pen or a
highlighter) that enables you to draw on a particular slide, enabling
you to quickly emphasize a particular point visually. Other features
include the ability to add speaking notes on the fly as you view the

presentation. You can also blank out the current slide to a black or white screen, allowing you to pause for a moment and answer audience questions or comments.

These tools are accessed by clicking on the icons that appear on the bottom left of your presentation slides as you show the presentation. There is an icon for the pen feature and a second icon that brings up a menu that allows you to access screen settings and a Go To feature that allows you to quickly go to a particular slide in the presentation. We discuss the use of the pen, speaker notes, and the Go to feature in the sections that follow.

Timesaver tip

Access the Slide Show Icons   If you move the mouse over a slide being shown in the Slide Show window, a series of buttons appear on the bottom left side of the slide pane.

Drawing with a Pen

12

An extremely useful tool is the pen, which enables you to draw on a particular slide. This is great for highlighting information on a slide to emphasize a particular point.

To use the pen during the slide show, follow these steps:

1 With the slide show running, click on the Pen icon that appears on the bottom left of the current slide.

2 On the menu that appears, select one of the pen types such as the **Ball Point Pen**. The mouse pointer becomes a ball point pen. (You can also choose to use a felt tip pen or a highlighter.)

3 Click the left mouse button and draw on the slide as needed (see Figure 12.4).

4 After you've finished working with the pen, you can return to the arrow pointer. Click the **Pen** icon. Select **Arrow** on the menu that appears. You can now use the mouse to advance to the next slide.

You can also choose the pen color that you use to draw on the slides. After clicking on the **Pen** icon, point at **Ink Color**, and then select the pen color you want to use from the color palette that appears.

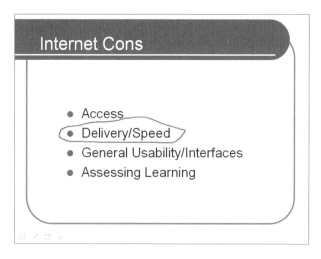

Figure 12.4 The pen provides you with an easy way to highlight a particular item on a slide.

Taking Speaker Notes

Another useful tool that you can take advantage of while showing your slide presentation is the Speaker Notes feature. It enables you to quickly take notes related to the discussion or to audience comments made during your presentation.

To use the Speaker Notes feature, follow these steps:

1 With the slide show running, point at the **Menu** icon on the bottom left of the current slide (it is the third icon from the left).

2 On the menu that appears, point at **Screen** and then select **Speaker Notes**. The Speaker Notes dialog box opens (see Figure 12.5).

3 Type your notes into the Speaker Notes dialog box.

4 When you have finished adding notes, click the **Close** button to close the dialog box.

Finding a Particular Slide During the Show

As you reach the end of a presentation, you might be asked to reshow a particular slide or subset of slides that you included in your slide show. The easiest way to go to a particular slide when you are in the Slide Show view is to use the Go to Slide command on the Slide Show menu.

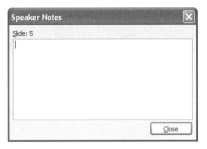

Figure 12.5 The Speaker Notes box allows you to record notes related to the current slide.

To go to a particular slide in the presentation, follow these steps:

1 With the slide show running, click the Menu button on the bottom left of the current slide.

2 On the menu that appears, point at **Go to Slide**. A submenu will appear showing all the slides (titles) in the presentation (see Figure 12.6).

3 To move to a particular slide, click the slide's title on the submenu. PowerPoint takes you to the selected slide.

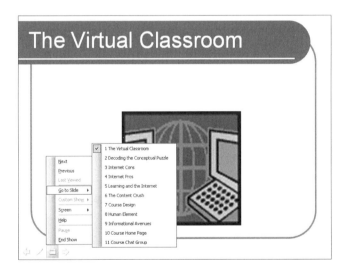

Figure 12.6 You can quickly go to any slide in the presentation.

→ Adding Action Buttons to User-Interactive Shows

You can create slide show presentations that will be played on a computer where your audience actually interacts with the slide show (for example, a computer at a trade show that tells potential customers about your company). This means that you need to give the audience some means of controlling the show. You can simply provide access to a keyboard and/or mouse and let the user control the show in the same way you learned earlier in this lesson, or you can provide action buttons onscreen that make it easy to jump to specific slides.

Action buttons are like controls on an audio CD player; they enable you to jump to any slide quickly, to go backward, to go forward, or even to stop the presentation.

Timesaver tip

The Same Controls on All Slides? If you want to add the same action buttons to all slides in the presentation, add the action buttons to the Slide Master. To display the Slide Master, select **View**, point at **Master**, and then choose **Slide Master**.

To add an action button to a slide, follow these steps.

1 Display the slide in Normal view.

2 Select **Slide Show**, point at **Action Buttons**, and pick a button from the palette that appears. For example, if you want to create a button that advances to the next slide, you might choose the button with the arrow pointing to the right.

Timesaver tip

Which Button Should I Choose? Consider the action that you want the button to perform, and then pick a button picture that matches it well. To change the button picture, you must delete the button and create a new one.

3 Your mouse pointer turns into a crosshair. Drag to draw a box on the slide where you want the button to appear. (You can resize it later if you want.) PowerPoint draws the button on the slide and opens the Action Settings dialog box (see Figure 12.7).

Figure 12.7 Set the action for your button in the Action Settings dialog box.

4 Select either the **Mouse Click** tab or **Mouse Over** tab to set the action for the button (Mouse Click options require a click; Mouse Over requires only that the mouse pointer be placed on the button).

5 Choose the type of action you want to happen when the user clicks the button. Click the **Hyperlink To** drop-down list and select an action such as **Next Slide**.

6 (Optional) If you want a sound to play when the user clicks the button, select the **Play Sound** check box and choose a sound from the drop-down list.

7 Click **OK**. Your button appears on the slide.

8 View the presentation (as you learned at the beginning of this lesson) to try out the button.

If you do use buttons on your slides so that users can run the slide show, be sure you use the same style of button on each of your slides for a particular action. This kind of consistency gives the viewer of the presentation a feeling of comfort and control.

Timesaver tip

Buttons Can Do Many Things   You can also create action buttons that run a program or run a macro that has been created using the Visual Basic for Applications programming language. Although these are very advanced features not covered in this book, keep in mind as you learn more about PowerPoint that many possibilities exist for making very creative and complex slide show presentations.

→ Setting Slide Show Options

Depending on the type of show you're presenting, you might find it useful to make some adjustments to the way the show runs, such as making it run in a window (the default is full screen) or showing only certain slides. You'll find these controls and more in the Set Up Show dialog box, which you can open by clicking the **Slide Show** menu and selecting **Set Up Show** (see Figure 12.8).

Figure 12.8 Use the Set Up Show dialog box to give PowerPoint some basic instructions about how to present your slide show.

In this dialog box, you can choose from several options, including the following:

- Choose the medium for showing the presentation. Your choices are **Presented by a Speaker (Full Screen)**, **Browsed by an Individual (Window)**, and **Browsed at a Kiosk (Full Screen)**.

- Choose whether to loop the slide show continuously or to show it only once. You might want to loop it continuously so that it operates unaided at a kiosk at a trade show, for example.

- Show all the slides or a range of them (enter the range into the **From** and **To** boxes).

- Choose whether to advance slides manually or to use timings you set up.

- Choose a pen color. Use the Pen Color drop-down box to select a color.

Using the Set Up Show dialog box to set the various options for the show allows you to put the finishing touches on the presentation before you actually present it to your audience. For example, it negates the need to select a pen color on the fly, allowing you to concentrate on the slide content rather than trying to change the pen color with the audience watching.

This dialog box also allows you to set the viewing parameters for the environment that the presentation will be shown in. For example, if you are running the slideshow on a PC that will be used by individuals at a tradeshow booth, it makes sense to format the presentation to be viewed by an individual in a window. That way the individual can leave the presentation for a moment and take a look at any sample software or other items you have on the PC that support the presentation.

13 Printing Presentations, Notes, and Handouts

In this lesson, you learn how to select a size and orientation for the slides in your presentation and how to print the slides, notes, and handouts you create.

→ Using PowerPoint Notes and Handouts

Although PowerPoint presentations are designed to be shown on a computer screen, you might want to print some items related to the presentation. For example, as you design your presentation, you can enter notes related to each slide that you create in the Notes pane. These notes can then be printed out and used during the presentation.

Using speaker notes helps you keep on track during the presentation and provides you with the information that you want to present related to each slide in the presentation. When you print your notes, each slide is printed on a separate page with the notes printed below the slide.

If you want to make it easier for your audience to follow the presentation and perhaps take notes of their own, you can print out handouts. Handouts provide a hard copy of each slide. The number of slides printed on each page of the handout can range from 1 to 9 slides. If you choose to print three slides per page (this is set up in the Print dialog box, which is discussed later in this lesson), PowerPoint automatically places note lines on the printout pages to the right of each slide (which makes it even easier for your audience to take notes related to the slides in the presentation).

This lesson covers the options related to printing hard copies of your slides, notes, and handouts. Let's start with a look at printing out presentation slides.

→ Quick Printing with No Options

You can quickly print all the slides in the presentation. You don't get to make any decisions about your output, but you do get your printout without delay.

To print a quick copy of each slide in the presentation, choose one of these methods:

- Click the **Print** button on the Standard toolbar.
- Choose the **File** menu, choose **Print**, and click **OK**.
- Press **Ctrl+P** and click **OK**.

The downside of printing the presentation in this way is that you will get a printout of only one slide per page in the landscape orientation. It doesn't matter what view you are in—you just get the slides. This uses up a lot of printer ink or toner, and if you want to print the presentation as an outline or print the presentation so that you can see the presentation notes that you've made, you need to access printing options that provide more control over the printout.

One way to fine-tune some of the settings that control how pages will be printed is using the Page Setup dialog box.

→ Changing the Page Setup

The Page Setup dialog box enables you to select how slides, notes, and handouts should be oriented on the page (Portrait or Landscape) and the type of page that the slides should be formatted for, such as On-Screen Show, overhead sheets, or regular 8 1/2-inch by 11-inch paper.

To customize the Page Setup settings, follow these steps:

1 Select the **File** menu and select **Page Setup**. The Page Setup dialog box appears as shown in Figure 13.1.

2 Perform one of the following procedures to set the slide size:

- To use a standard size, select a size from the **Slides Sized For** drop-down list. For example, you can have slides sized for regular 8 1/2-inch by 11-inch paper, overheads, or 35mm slides (if you have a special printer that can create slides).
- To create a custom size, enter the dimensions into the **Width** and **Height** text boxes.

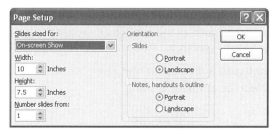

Figure 13.1 The Page Setup dialog box enables you to set the paper type and the orientation of slides and notes on the page.

Timesaver tip

Spin Boxes The arrows to the right of the Width and Height text boxes enable you to adjust the settings in those boxes. Click the up arrow to increase the setting by .1 inch or the down arrow to decrease it by .1 inch.

3 In the **Number Slides From** text box, type the number with which you want to start numbering slides. (This is usually **1**, but you might want to start with a different number if the presentation is a continuation of another.)

4 Under the Slides heading, choose **Portrait** or **Landscape** orientation for your slides.

5 In the Notes, Handouts & Outline section, choose **Portrait** or **Landscape** for those items.

6 Click **OK**. If you changed the orientation of your slides, you might have to wait a moment while PowerPoint repositions the slides.

→ Choosing What and How to Print

To really control your printouts related to a particular presentation, use the various options supplied in the Print dialog box. The Print dialog box enables you to specify what to print, such as handouts or the presentation as an outline; it also enables you to specify the printer to use for the printout. For example, you might want to use a color printer for overhead transparencies and a black-and-white printer for your handouts. To set your print options, follow these steps:

1 Select the **File** menu and select **Print**. The Print dialog box appears with the name of the currently selected printer in the Name box (see Figure 13.2).

2 If you want to use a different printer, open the Name drop-down list and select the printer you want.

Timesaver tip

Printer Properties The Properties button enables you to adjust graphics quality, select paper size, and choose which paper tray to use, among other things.

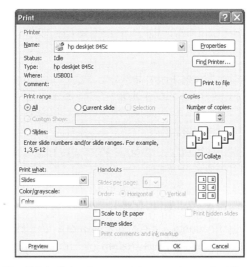

Figure 13.2 **The Print dialog box enables you to control the printer and the printouts.**

3 Choose what to print in the Print Range section:

■ Choose **All** to print all the slides in the presentation.

■ Choose **Current Slide** to print only the currently displayed slide.

■ Enter a range of slide numbers into the **Slides** text box; for example, enter **2–4** to print slides 2, 3, and 4.

4 Open the **Print What** drop-down list and choose what you want to print. You can print slides, handouts, notes, or outlines.

5 If you want more than one copy, enter the number of copies you want into the **Number of Copies** box.

6 Use the Color/Grayscale drop-down box to specify whether the printout should be in color, grayscale, or black and white.

7 If you are printing handouts, use the Handouts box to specify the number of slides that should be printed per page and the orientation used for the printed page (Portrait or Landscape).

8 Select or deselect any of these check boxes in the dialog box, as required:

- Print to File—Select this option to send the output to a file rather than to your printer.

- Collate—If you are printing more than one copy, select this check box to collate (1, 2, 3, 1, 2, 3) each printed copy instead of printing all the copies of each page at once (1, 1, 2, 2, 3, 3).

- Scale to Fit Paper—If the slide (or whatever you're printing) is too large to fit on the page, select this check box to decrease the size of the slide to make it fit on the page. Now you won't have to paste two pieces of paper together to see the whole slide.

- Frame Slides—Select this check box if you want to print a border around each slide.

- Print Hidden Slides—If you have any hidden slides, you can choose whether to print them. If you don't have any hidden slides, this check box will be unavailable.

- Print Comments and Ink Markup—Prints all the comments on the slides of the presentation on a separate comments page. This option also prints any ink markups that you have made using the pen feature when viewing the presentation.

Timesaver tip

Preview Your Printout Selection After specifying the various options in the Print dialog box, you might want to preview the printout before you send it to the printer. Click the **Preview** button. You are taken to the Print Preview screen. If things look good on the Print Preview screen, click **Print** to send the printout to the printer.

9 Click **OK** to print.